2/02

3000 800052 87670
St. Louis Community College

Meramec Library
St. Louis Community College
11333 Big Bend Blvd.
Kirkwood, MO 63122-5799
314-984-7797

WITHDRAWN

D1379306

St. Louis Community College
at Meramec
Library

INDUSTRY, ARCHITECTURE, AND ENGINEERING

INDUSTRY, ARCHITECTURE, AND ENGINEERING

LOUIS BERGERON

MARIA TERESA MAIULLARI-PONTOIS

Foreword by Eric DeLony

Translated by Jane Marie Todd

HARRY N. ABRAMS, INC., PUBLISHERS

Contents

Page 2: *Forging a shaft under a thirteen-thousand-ton press in Bethlehem, Pennsylvania.*

Above: *A fresco (1959) by Frank Ashley depicts labor in the sawmills and shipyards of the Pacific Coast Steel Company. The work is reminiscent of Diego Rivera's famous cycle of frescoes (1932–33) devoted to the automobile industry, executed for the River Rouge plant and now located at the Detroit Institute of Arts.*

Overleaf: *Locomotive at the Bethlehem factory in Pennsylvania.*

American Industrial Archaeology

ERIC DELONY

Timing is everything. If this is true, then for those of us who discovered industrial archaeology in the late 1960s and early 1970s (this includes people from all nations, not just America), our timing was perfect. Though much of the technological heritage of Europe and the United States had been lost during the twentieth century through natural attrition, global conflicts, and, in America, the scrap drives of two world wars, an abundance of industrial and engineering artifacts still dotted the landscapes on both continents. These artifacts were awaiting identification, evaluation, and, when possible, preservation and interpretation. Countries throughout the world retained a wealth of bridges, dams, canals, factories, power plants, and other engineering and industrial resources of historical interest.

Those of us who discovered industrial archaeology during this period were fortunate, for we were the pioneers who enjoyed the thrill of discovery—of identifying a new type of monument and then having the responsibility of convincing the rest of the world that these resources had value and that selected examples should be saved for posterity. We also were challenged to invent new strategies for relating these newly discovered resources to the rest of the built architectural environment that historians, architects, and preservationists were struggling to save.[1] Even though a wealth of sites, structures, and objects survived, we realized that the future held little hope that all industrial sites could be saved as historic monuments. Considering the geometrically increasing rate at which much of our historic architecture was being lost to the onslaught of "progress" in the form of post–World War II rebuilding, freeway construction, and urban renewal, industrial archaeologists were quick to point out that the destruction of engineering and industrial resources was occurring at a higher rate than the attrition of architectural monuments. Factories, machines, bridges, and the other relics of engineering and industry were simply not regarded as historic, much less worth saving. However, it was not too unrealistic to expect that selected sites could be rehabilitated or adaptively reused. There were even visions that entire industrial landscapes could be preserved as museum villages or historic districts.

Aerial view of the deck of the Throgs Neck Bridge, The Bronx, New York.

At the same time, planners and developers, in concert with engineers and architects, were rebuilding cities devastated by war and, on both continents, installing the greatest road system since the Romans. While the majority of citizens applauded this work, others perceived the freeways and urban renewal projects as destroyers of cities, bifurcating neighborhoods and desecrating wilderness. In short, the planners, architects, and engineers working on these projects were viewed as heartless—anesthetized to historic structures and the natural environment.[2] Preservation through documentation was possible, however, and one of the first official recognitions that industrial archaeology existed in the United States came in 1969 when the United States Congress established the Historic American Engineering Record (HAER). HAER was the last program established as part of the new preservation movement in America. Since then, HAER and industrial archaeologists have worked to create a national documentation program of America's industrial, engineering, and technological achievements. Some of the sites recorded have served as the foundation for subsequent preservation efforts that transformed communities and the way people think of the industrial workplace.

This essay is not a history of HAER, rather, it is a personal reflection on American industrial archaeology by one who was in the right place at the right time, who caught that initial wave of enthusiasm and discovery, and has ridden it for the last thirty years. I mention HAER because it is the organization with which I have been affiliated for three decades, and it provides the context from which I have experienced industrial archaeology. It is in large part the reason this book is being published—most of the illustrations are from the HAER collection.[3]

One cannot attempt to cover all aspects of the American industrial archaeology movement in a short essay. I will endeavor to highlight several of the important benchmarks and some of the key events that have shaped the field. The first thirty years of the movement can be broken down into two phases: from 1969 to 1979, a decade of discovery, invention, and proselytizing a new field of heritage preservation; and from 1980 to the present, a period of steady growth, recognition, and the salvation of selected sites. In thirty years, American industrial archaeologists have succeeded in their mission by expanding the vision of historic preservation to include sites, structures, and objects of engineering and industry. Since 1969, nearly seven thousand industrial sites have been recorded with photographs, measured and interpretive drawings, and histories. Along with documentation, there has been significant national legislation passed that protects the cultural patrimony, including industrial sites. Numerous cooperative relationships have been forged between federal, state, and local governments, as well as private citizens and private industry to save industrial monuments. We have adopted an entrepreneurial philosophy for greater flexibility. Numerous educational programs and seminars have been established to train individuals interested in practicing industrial archaeology and to inform the public about their industrial heritage. All these activities have had moderate success in saving both the outstanding, nationally significant, monumental sites, and the more representational examples of state or local significance that contribute substantially to a vernacular vocabulary and compose most of the components of historic industrial districts.

But before getting into specific examples, it is important to understand how industrial archaeology arrived in the United States. The American movement was initiated primarily through the efforts of Robert M. Vogel, former curator of mechanical and civil engineering at the Museum of History and Technology, Smithsonian Institution. He was part of that initial group who caught the first wave of discovery by attending some of the world's first industrial archaeology conferences, organized in England by Kenneth Hudson and Angus Buchanan at Bath University of Technology. It should not be surprising that industrial archaeology got its start in the United Kingdom. Britain can rightfully claim to have originated the field since it is generally recognized as the birthplace of the industrial revolution. Subsequently, Vogel convened a similar seminar at the Smithsonian on April 11, 1967, where a number of ideas and individuals coalesced to launch the American equivalent of an industrial archaeology movement based in part on British practice. Two years later, these efforts bore fruit with the establishment of the Historic American Engineering Record, followed in 1971 by the founding of the Society for Industrial Archeology (SIA), with Vogel as the editor of

the *SIA Newsletter* and Ted Sande, its first president. Much could be gained from legitimatizing the new field of study, and so, in addition to the enactment of HAER, opportunities were created to ensure that the subject was introduced and debated. This pattern was repeated in countries throughout the industrialized world. It soon became evident that all countries could benefit by learning from each other's experiences. In 1972, the first international industrial archaeology conference was hosted, appropriately by England, at the recently created Ironbridge Gorge Museum in the Severn River valley in Shropshire. Ever since, international conferences on the subject have been convened triennially, hosted by different countries throughout the world.

Returning to the United States, another important mandate that weighed heavily in the early success of industrial archaeology and, for that matter, the entire historic preservation movement in America, was the 1966 Historic Preservation Act, which was passed toward the end of President Lyndon Johnson's administration. This important legislation established a federal/state partnership to preserve the national patrimony. The 1966 act was considerably enhanced in May 1971, when President Richard M. Nixon signed Executive Order 11593. It mandated that if any building, site, structure, or object listed or eligible for listing on the National Register of Historic Places were threatened by a federally funded or licensed project, federal agencies were required to follow a procedure to mitigate the effects of its activities on the historic resource. The provisions of Executive Order 11593 mandated federal stewardship and responsibility of historic resources and later became law under the National Historic Preservation Act Amendments of 1980.[4]

While it is significant that after nearly thirty years of preservation efforts few sites of national significance, regardless of whether they are industrial or architectural, are being destroyed, it is not accurate to claim that industrial heritage is a mainstream concern of the American public. However, at least industrial archaeology is recognized as part of the larger spectrum of the preservation movement. In addition to the support the field receives from the National Park Service, the Smithsonian Institution, the Library of Congress, and the Society for Industrial Archeology, it enjoys the advocacy of other partners such as historical societies, private industry, individuals, and community groups. Professional organizations such as the American Society of Civil Engineers and the American Institute of Architects have history and heritage committees as part of their agendas. Both organizations have landmark designation programs and promote awareness and appreciation of their respective histories throughout the profession and externally to the public. Federal agencies and state and local governments are required by law to take industrial heritage into account as part of their daily activities, and each state has a program responsible for promoting preservation at the state level. Not relying exclusively on one federal group or funding source gives the movement great flexibility. The success of American industrial archaeology is based on the premise that all sectors of society—government, business, industry, and individuals—must participate in a national preservation effort. Participation, especially financial, doubles and sometimes triples the effect of the program. More importantly, it encourages partners to recognize the concept of industrial heritage and, by extension, fosters a commitment to preserving significant attributes of the industrial and engineered environment.

1969–1979: A DECADE OF DISCOVERY AND EXPERIMENTATION

The first ten years of industrial archaeology in America can be characterized as exploratory, looking at as diverse a group of sites, structures, and artifacts as possible, and trying different techniques of research, documentation, and graphic interpretation. Since little was known of engineering and industrial works, industrial archaeologists began preparing site-specific inventories. The network of state historic preservation offices in the United States, working with HAER and with universities and other preservation groups, initiated a series of inventory projects. State inventories were conducted in Virginia, Pennsylvania, Florida, Oklahoma, California, Delaware, South Dakota, Colorado, Georgia, Michigan, and Rhode Island, and area inventories in Trenton, New Jersey; Cuyahoga County, Ohio; western New York State; and the lower Merrimack Valley in New England.[5] It soon became ap-

parent, however, that a national inventory of all industrial sites was unrealistic in a country as vast and diversified as the United States. Nonetheless, the dozen or so inventories that were completed served to introduce industrial and engineering properties so that they would be included in more general cultural-resource surveys being conducted by the state preservation programs.

While the inventories were ongoing, a number of practitioners started doing individual site documentation. A multitude of threats demanded that specific sites be recorded regardless of whether there was any established hierarchy of importance. It soon became apparent that skills in many disciplines were needed to understand large, complex industrial sites. Those sites that survived into the 1970s had undergone many changes, resulting in layers of additions or partial removal of structures. Deciphering these changes required skillful practitioners in many fields—architects, engineers, historians, industrial designers, archaeologists, enthusiasts, and photographers—anyone who could contribute was encouraged to enter the field. Success at understanding complex industrial sites requires a multidisciplinary team with a site-specific focus, and this approach remains the fundamental day-to-day philosophy of American industrial archaeology.

To arrest the tide of massive destruction wrought by urban renewal and the interstate highway system, industrial archaeologists also began addressing the more complex problems of helping revitalize depressed industrial districts. Paterson, New Jersey, and Lowell, Massachusetts, were two of the first former industrial cities to be investigated. Both areas claim "birthplace" status as the origin of America's Industrial Revolution. Paterson was established in the late eighteenth century by Alexander Hamilton as the first planned industrial district. Designed by Pierre Charles L'Enfant, the planner of the nation's capital, the city was laid out around a three-tiered system of canals that ran factories and mills by water power. These included the first Colt firearms works, early locomotive manufactories, and, by the late nineteenth century, mills that eventually distinguished Paterson as the silk capital of the world. Lowell, located at the falls of the Merrimack River in Massachusetts, also used a three-tiered hydraulic canal system to power cotton mills. It became an important center of the American

textile industry and, by the Civil War, the largest textile-producing center in the world. Both communities began deteriorating when their industries moved south during the early twentieth century. In the late 1960s and early 1970s, Paterson and Lowell represented the epitome of depressed industrial towns: thousands of square feet of underutilized mill buildings and factory floors, deteriorating center cities, an aging workforce mixed with a growing minority population, and, in Paterson, a 1950s solution to urban decay: building an interstate-scale highway through the heart of the crumbling industrial district. Working with local leaders, industrial archaeologists sought to establish these cities as distinctive historic areas, based not on contemporary urban renewal tenets of mass clearing and new construction, but by building on the themes of the city's existing industrial heritage. Emptied canals were restored as linear parks that linked neighborhoods together, and abandoned mills and factory buildings, rather than being destroyed, were adaptively reused. To this day, Paterson and Lowell continue in this vein. Paterson was designated a National Historic Landmark in 1976, and Lowell's historic core gained the distinction of National Historical Park status in 1978.

The 1970s were capped by a new type of project and the radical reorganization of federal preservation programs. In 1977 "rehab-action" began. A program envisioned to expand the documentation mandate by including a planning element, it was designed to identify adaptive reuses for industrial buildings and strategies for revitalizing depressed industrial towns. Rehab-action was based on two initiatives of the Carter administration—rehabilitation tax incentives and energy conservation. The 1976 Tax Act, which promised tax incentives for owners who rehabilitated their buildings according to the Secretary of the Interior's standards, became the largest source of funding in the history of the preservation movement up to that time. Thousands of projects worth many millions of dollars were completed based on an incentive in the legislation that allowed commercial property owners to deduct up to twenty-five percent of the rehabilitation costs if the property was eligible for the National Register and met the rehabilitation standards. Coupled with the tax incentives was energy-efficiency legislation that President Carter succeeded in passing in reaction to the Arab oil crisis of the early 1970s. This legislation offered tax incentives to property owners

"Bridge 28" is one of the five cast-iron bridges in Central Park in New York City. Designed by Calvert Vaux and Jacob Wrey Mould in 1864, this footbridge is notable for its use of cast iron, rarely used in the United States before that time, and for its unusual design, which anticipates the appearance of the Art Nouveau style by a quarter century.

who invested in energy-efficient technologies for both new construction and adaptive reuse and rehabilitation work.

While federal legislation ensured that sites of state or local significance impacted by federal actions were protected, success would be limited unless there was a strong local presence to speak out for industrial heritage. This level of involvement has developed over the last two decades. SIA, through its many chapters across the United States, provides a local constituency at the grass roots. America's industrial archaeologists had to concentrate on building a national constituency to assuage the threats not only to sites of national significance, but also to sites of state or local interest.

1984–PRESENT: MATURATION

Ironically, much of the threat to America's industrial archaeology can be attributed to deteriorating public works and infrastructure, and to the process of deindustrialization. The need to upgrade America's highways and public works—water, sewage, and hydroelectric generating plants, for example—has placed great pressure on recording these sites before they are altered or destroyed. Most were built in the last quarter of the nineteenth or first quarter of the twentieth century. While not all these sites retain historic machinery, many qualify for recording. Deindustrialization, rebuilding the nation's highways, and rationalizing the rail infrastructure have placed many of America's industrial buildings, historic bridges, and rail facilities at risk.

One of the first structural types of national significance to illustrate the rapidly deteriorating infrastructure was America's bridges. When the Federal Highway Administration launched the Bridge Replacement and Rehabilitation Program following the collapse of the Silver Bridge over the Ohio River in 1967, HAER, though only recently established, realized that the dwindling stock of historic metal-truss bridges would be the first to go and launched one of its first comprehensive, national programs to protect historic bridges, beginning in 1973. This was a carefully crafted and orchestrated strategy developed in cooperation with the National Trust for Historic Preservation, the Advisory Council on Historic Preservation, and the state historic preservation

offices. Its first goal was to promote comprehensive inventories of historic bridges within each state. By the time inventories were required by law (1987), most states had completed some form of historic bridge survey, and bridges became the first class of historic structures to be nationally evaluated.[6] Following the inventory and evaluation phase, HAER returned to those states that had identified outstanding collections of historic bridges and began their systematic recording. Many states have adopted bridge preservation or management plans that provide some degree of protection. So pervasive is the effect of transportation on the cultural landscape, I have always believed that if we succeeded involving transportation interests in historic preservation, we stood a much better chance of success.

When HAER proposed its historic bridges program, the initial reaction of the Federal Highway Administration and state departments of transportation was adversarial. The perception of highway planners and engineers was one of conflicting mandates. On the one hand they were being told to upgrade a deteriorating highway system while at the same time they had to repair and rehabilitate historic bridges that rarely complied with modern design and safety standards. It soon became evident, however, that there never would be sufficient funding to replace every functionally obsolete and structurally deficient bridge with a new structure. Rehabilitation was one of the viable alternatives. As the inventories began to reveal the wealth of historic bridges still standing, some engineers came to appreciate their value. They realized that not every bridge needed to be upgraded to interstate standards. Skilled engineers were able to develop rehabilitation designs that maintained the historic characteristics of the bridges while at the same time allowing for reasonable safety. Some states have even dedicated a portion of their rehabilitation funds to preserve their truly outstanding historic bridges.[7]

Bridges do not exist in isolation historically or physically. Roads, one of the important contexts for bridges, have played a significant role in the development of the American cultural landscape. A wonderful network of secondary farm roads continues to be popular for Sunday leisure driving. In many parts of the United States, touring the countryside represents thousands of tourist dollars. Historic bridges are an important feature of that experience; while nostalgic wooden covered bridges have always been popular, there is a growing interest in the concrete arches and metal-truss spans that reveal the story of American inventiveness and manufacturing ingenuity. For bridges that cannot be continued in vehicular service, a viable alternative is relocation to roads that receive less traffic, or for use on forest inspection and maintenance roads. Historic bridges can be used on hiking paths and bike trails in local, state, and national parks. They have even been used on golf courses and cattle ranches.

As both the states and the National Park Service invest millions of dollars upgrading the country's highway infrastructure, these initiatives had to cover many criteria. Their purpose was to save representative examples of America's historic bridges, to encourage the recognition of scenic country roads and urban parkways, and, if new construction or rehabilitation was required, to encourage quality design that took aesthetics, the historic roadway, and landscape characteristics into consideration. There has been a significant shift in the perception and attitudes of engineers and highway planners toward historic roads and bridges. HAER, the National Trust, and many of the state preservation offices now are working in alliance with engineers to bring quality design and excellence to America's highway systems.

Other areas in which American industrial archaeologists have focused their efforts since the mid-1980s are maritime, military, and hard-rock mining resources. In 1985, the National Trust for Historic Preservation, attuned to the national interest in tall ships first inspired during America's bicentennial celebration in 1976, initiated a new program of documenting historic ships and other maritime resources like lighthouses, marine railways, and related features. Since the first ship, *Wawona,* was documented by HAER in Seattle harbor in 1985, many other vessels have received similar treatment.

Among the effects of the termination of the Cold War has been base closures and modernization of our defense resources. HAER had documented sites such as the Picatinny Arsenal and other munitions development, research, and storage installations. New projects have been conducted at the Navy's aeronautical research and engineering facilities in Langley, Virginia, at Wright-Patterson Air Force Base, in Dayton, Ohio, and at the Philadelphia Navy Yard.

With liberal laws for mining on federal land, new technologies for extracting gold, and continued high prices for the metal, what little remains of historic hard-rock mining resources, especially in the western states, is in jeopardy. In cooperation with Death Valley National Monument superintendent, Edwin Rothfuss, Robert Spude of the Park Service's Rocky Mountain Regional Office, Ann Huston and Leo Barker in San Francisco, and mining historians and archaeologists throughout the West, HAER organized a week-long historic mining workshop in Death Valley in 1989. From this developed HAER's Hard-Rock Mining Initiative, which has placed a priority on mining resources by developing cooperative recording projects with the mining industry, state and national parks, state preservation offices, and the mining archaeology and history groups.

Deindustrialization has had a powerful impact since the 1980s as America, like other modern nations, moved from being a manufacturing to a service economy. The miles of magnificent steel mills, blast furnaces, and coke plants along the Monongahela River around Pittsburgh, for over a century the world's image of America's industrial strength, no longer exist. The same holds true for New England's textile industry, the anthracite regions of northeastern Pennsylvania, and the hard-rock mining fields of the West. Even the physical artifacts of America's space program—"One small step for man, one giant step for mankind"—such as Rocket Row at Cape Canaveral, are being reclaimed by Everglades-like jungles and a severe marine environment. Large, complex industrial sites, particularly those with rapidly evolving technologies, are extremely susceptible to functional, technological, and economic obsolescence. Increasingly, this will happen before the sites reach fifty years of age, when they are old enough to be considered historic by National Register criteria. Most will simply vanish without a trace unless HAER can record them.

As formerly thriving communities become depressed when industries relocate, deindustrialization has stirred local congressmen to help identify alternative employment opportunities for their constituents. One alternative is *heritage tourism.* Depressed,

The factory of the Seneca Glass Company, in the heart of Morgantown, West Virginia, was renovated and reused as a site for exhibiting crystal and as a restaurant. The stout, conical brick smokestack and modern electric plant in the background are symbolic of the shift from one era to the next.

15

"rust-belt" communities striving to end their downward spiral have discovered the potential of heritage tourism, a concept not entirely new. Though places like Williamsburg, Old Sturbridge Village, Plymouth Plantation, and Deerfield, Massachusetts, had been established in the early twentieth century, and historic districts such as those in Charleston, South Carolina, Savannah, Georgia, and the Vieux Carré in New Orleans had existed for many decades, hundreds of new historic districts were established in towns throughout the United States as a result of state-sponsored National Register surveys and nominations.

For much of the public and many in the National Park Service, Yellowstone will forever be the ideal of a national park in the United States—a federal precinct carved out of the wilderness where people can commune with nature. However, because of economic limitations, many Americans are unable to enjoy a national park experience, and, for others, such an experience may hold little relevance. Since the 1960s, the park service has become the sometimes reluctant caretaker not just of new natural parks but of new kinds of parks. These were a new generation of urban parks that gave Americans a chance to discover their history and culture, not just pristine wilderness.

Stemming from the influence of the "new preservation," Congress had been persuaded that architectural and cultural sites were as worthy of commemoration as battlefields and places of scenic beauty. In 1972, the first urban parks were created with the establishment of the Gateway and Golden Gate National Recreation Areas in New York and New Jersey, and San Francisco, respectively. By the late 1970s, "heritage areas" like Lowell (1978) were another new kind of park.[8] What was innovative about the concept

of heritage areas and corridors was that it is interdisciplinary, calling for the integration of preservation and conservation, and for the protection of entire geographic regions, with the buildings, landscapes, and lifestyles they encompass. For industrial archaeologists, many of the new heritage areas considered as significant and worthy of preservation include canal, rail, and transportation corridors and industrial districts. Paterson and Lowell were two of the first to pioneer the concept, but by the mid-1980s, dozens of other communities began looking to the National Park Service for help in redeveloping their decaying neighborhoods and industrial cores. Park Service funding, directed to these locales by local congressmen through the appropriation process, have provided a whisper of hope that these dying towns could be revived. Presently, there are about a dozen of these areas in various stages of planning and development and another ten were designated by Congress in 1996.

Not all sites, no matter how worthy, can be owned and administrated by the National Park Service. For some, the solution lies with the creation of a local and state partnership that administers a heritage area commission with technical assistance from the National Park Service. Sites designated as national heritage areas include the Illinois & Michigan Canal National Heritage Corridor. It was followed by America's Industrial Heritage Project (AIHP) and the Lehigh & Delaware Canal National Heritage Corridor, an area more than 150 miles in length along the Lehigh and Delaware rivers, from the anthracite coal fields in northeastern Pennsylvania to the former "workshop of the world"—Philadelphia. The Blackstone River Valley National Heritage Corridor, a fifty-mile stretch in Rhode Island and Massachusetts that seeks to preserve remnants of the southern New England textile industry, is characterized by tightly knit nineteenth-century mill hamlets that dot the countryside along this former industrial and transportation corridor. Though not yet officially designated, the citizens of Birmingham, Alabama, saved the Sloss Furnaces in the 1970s and, under the leadership of Marjorie Longnecker White, president of the Birmingham Historical Society, now are working to save and interpret related aspects of the iron, coal, and mining industries of the five-county area surrounding Birmingham, the cast-iron center of the world.

The newly designated areas include the Augusta Canal National Heritage Area (Georgia), America's Agricultural Heritage Partnership (Iowa); to be administered by the U.S. Department of Agriculture, the National Coal Heritage Area (West Virginia), the Essex National Heritage Area (Massachusetts), the Hudson River Valley National Heritage Area (New York), the Ohio & Erie Canal National Heritage Corridor (Ohio), the South Carolina National Heritage Corridor, the Steel Industry American Heritage Area (Pennsylvania), and the Tennessee Civil War Heritage Area. Setting aside selected sites for future interpretation as industrial or open-air museums is one option. Others include finding alternative uses for the industrial buildings and public works. Both strategies have worked successfully in American cities to varying degrees, but industrial heritage areas and corridors are one of the most inspiring and exciting initiatives to emerge in recent years.

The industrial heritage area is a ten-year phenomenon that holds great promise for the future. For the first time, a mechanism has been created that offers a chance of working where amenities in the form of natural, recreational, and cultural resources are weighed and evaluated equitably with the other forces driving development. Community leaders cannot deny that these resources are worth preserving. In many communities, citizens now insist that these values be included in any redevelopment scheme.

Features and attributes, manmade and natural, are what distinguish one community from another, offering identity and a sense of place. Historic buildings and neighborhoods of varied textures that perpetuate the human scale are becoming more and more the primary components that planners and developers use to revitalize communities. The American public is becoming more sophisticated, realizing that the destruction of old buildings and the replacement of green space and waterfronts with seamless shopping malls and suburban developments are no longer the only options.

THE NEW MILLENNIUM

I see no reason that interest in engineering and industrial heritage should abate in the future. The growth curve that the field of industrial archaeology has experienced over the last decade should continue upward. The public is realizing the value of the contribution that American technology has made toward world development. Threats from infrastructure rehabilitation, deindustrialization, and continued suburbanization will be mitigated, the most important remnants of industry and engineering will continue to be scrutinized, and, hopefully, the most significant sites preserved. Nonetheless, eternal vigilance is the price of victory, no matter the cause. Preservationists, industrial archaeologists, and ordinary citizens must speak out when our fragile built environment—regardless of whether it is architectural, vernacular, or industrial—is threatened. Selective recording is especially important for the heritage at risk. These are the industries and public works undergoing drastic change: coal and hard-rock mining, water supply and sanitation, hydroelectric generation, railroads, and maritime transportation. Documentation must be completed on the "anachronistic industries," not candlemaking or basketweaving, but industries such as the Seneca Glass Works or the Bretz coke ovens in West Virginia, that, having survived modernization and redundancy, should be targeted for recording, preservation, and interpretation as past examples of the American workplace.[9]

Other areas where industrial archaeologists have had limited involvement include the mining fields in the Midwest and mountain areas and the centers of heavy industry—particularly Philadelphia, Chicago, Gary, Milwaukee, St. Louis, Kansas City, Denver, Portland, and Los Angeles—where disproportionately few sites have been recorded in comparison to the potential richness and significance of the industrial resources in these cities.

One possible solution to address continued threats is for Society for Industrial Archeology members, state preservation offices, and HAER to target particular states, groups, and aca-

The thermal electric plant in Port Richmond, northeast of Philadelphia. Built in 1925, it is the last of a series of five plants built by the Philadelphia Electric Company.

demic institutions to develop contextual studies for various structure types and industrial landscapes. With such studies in hand, it then is possible to address classes of resources that are not adequately represented. The incidence of "eleventh-hour" campaigns to preserve sites under threat could be reduced if industrial archeology and preservation authorities implemented a proactive program of nominating engineering and industrial sites in their areas to the National Register. HAER has initiated efforts in this direction by its work on bridges and its ongoing study of blast furnaces. Contextual studies will accelerate the identification of priorities for recording and protection.

In addition, the appreciation and awareness of engineering and industrial heritage must be developed in institutions of higher education. Technological heritage should be integrated into the curricula of architecture, material culture, history of technology, and historic preservation. Particularly important is that engineers take a larger stake in preserving the outstanding physical remnants of their profession.

The success of industrial archaeology demanded that engineers get involved and play a major part in the movement. Some have always been interested in the history of civil engineering and had worked to establish a history program within the American Society of Civil Engineers. Only recently have other engineers begun to share this vision of the future development of America. Forums such as the annual meetings of the American Society of Civil Engineers, the American Society of Mechanical Engineers, and the SIA offer the opportunity to inform engineers of their past achievements so they can make choices based not only on the bottom line but on aesthetics and quality-of-life issues as well. Since much of our historic built environment is the product of engineers, its conscientious maintenance and preservation requires their expertise and insights. We need not just any engineers but specialists who are familiar with the materials, formulas, and practices of their predecessors, so they can craft solutions that respect the character and qualities of past achievements.

America's collaboration with industrial archaeologists in other countries has taught us that we live in a global community that continues to shrink at alarming rates. Much can be learned from work in other countries. I have been fortunate to represent the United States at several triennial meetings of The International Committee for the Conservation of the Industrial Heritage (TICCIH).[10] One of many things gleaned from TICCIH symposia is that the United States is not unique in its concern for industrial heritage. Most nations are acutely aware of their industrial heritage and are working to ensure its recognition and preservation. But what works for one country may not necessarily work for others. With varying governmental structures, legislation, and agendas, the means by which nations document and save industrial heritage differ.

This is more than just an enthusiast's pastime. When people ask me the value of industrial archaeology, I answer that we are in the amenity business, responsible for saving the very best handed down to us from the past so we can pass it on to the future. Preserving structures of fine materials, humanly scaled proportions, exceptional craftsmanship, and varied textures enhances the quality of life. In places where historic architecture, industry, and engineering are lacking, as one finds in many parts of the United States, attitudes supporting quality design may also be absent. Such values are especially needed in America, where we tend to throw away the past, build the expedient, pursue the quick profit, and, in the process, trash the countryside. In this age of instant gratification, suburbanization, and desecration of our urban cores and rural landscapes, industrial heritage and the other resources of the historic built environment provide a link with that past as well as deeper appreciation of the human imagination. Industrial archaeologists have tried to implant an ethic within the American public, that the oft-forgotten engineering structure or industrial workplace has significance and meaning. By extension, industrial heritage has the potential of involving working-class people, a sizeable segment of the population yet to be integrated into the preservation movement. By recognizing the industrial workplace we send the signal that the occupations of working-class people have value. We can all create a better environment through an appreciation of historic places, be they architectural, vernacular, or industrial, and thus enhance the quality of life for current and future generations.

1. It would be grossly inaccurate to suggest that engineering, industry, and technology had been totally ignored prior to this period. By 1970, more than sixty-eight engineering, industrial, and maritime sites had been recognized and commemorated as National Historic Landmarks, as national and state parks, or as historic sites. See the *Catalog of National Historic Landmarks, 1987*, compiled by the History Division, National Park Service, for a listing of all National Historic Landmarks designated through June 30, 1987.

2. Steve Lubar, "HABS/HAER/America's Industrial Heritage Project: Some Recent Publications," *The Public Historian* 13, no. 3 (summer 1991): 119; Samuel C. Florman, "The Humane Engineer: Greater Engineering," *Technology Review* 93, no. 5 (July 1990): 71.

3. The genesis of this book stems from an exhibition organized in 1997 by Louis Bergeron, former professor of economic history at the Ecole des Hautes Etudes dans les Sciences Sociales, Paris, and Dominique Ferriot, director of the Conservatoire Nationale des Arts et Métiers, also in Paris. Since retiring from academia, Dr. Bergeron was appointed president of the Ecomusée at Le Creusot-Montceau in the Burgundy region of France. He is also president of The International Congress for the Conservation of Industrial Heritage (TICCIH).

4. A significant spin-off of this and other environmental laws, such as the National Environmental Protection Act (NEPA), has been the employment of a vast community of consulting professionals, primarily archaeologists. Fieldwork in American archaeology gravitated toward cultural resource management, a bureaucratic term for the consideration, protection, and possible salvage of historic and prehistoric sites and structures in the path of oncoming federal projects. By 1978, the majority of funds for archaeological fieldwork was spent under the aegis of CRM. See Brenda Barrett, "IA's Role in the Cultural Resource Management," *Symposium: Industrial Archeology and the Human Sciences*, Dianne Newell, ed. (Washington, D.C.: Society for Industrial Archeology, 1977), 15.

6. The United States, like Western European countries, initiated national and regional inventories of historic industrial sites during the 1960s. Great Britain, recognizing its unique position as being the birthplace of the Industrial Revolution, developed one of the first comprehensive national inventory programs. Borrowing from the British precedent, America initiated a national inventory program. Sites identified were categorized by the HAER Industrial Classification, a system based on the U.S. Department of Commerce's standard industrial and land-use classification systems. The system was adapted for nineteenth- and early twentieth-century engineering and industrial works and was designed with eventual computerization in mind. User friendly, the classification codes are alpha-numeric, enabling name recognition of a particular industry or engineering work.

6. State historic bridge inventories, with few exceptions, do not include railroad bridges because the Federal Highway Administration and state transportation departments usually are concerned primarily with vehicular structures. The nation's railways, with the exception of Amtrak and Conrail, are privately owned, thus falling outside any federal purview so far as historic resources are concerned. It was the railroad industry, however, that pioneered most bridge technology in the second half of the nineteenth century. Until the current railroad industry recognizes the significance of its surviving bridges and agrees to assist in their evaluation and documentation, there remains a signifi-

cant gap in the history of American bridge technology. See Eric DeLony, "HAER's Historic Bridge Program," *IA: The Journal of the Society for Industrial Archeology* 15, no. 2 (1989): 57–71.

7. HAER's Park Roads and Bridges program taught us that, historically, the Park Service and the Bureau of Public Roads were partners in building the vast network of roads and bridges in the national park system. Park Service landscape architects provided standards and aesthetic guidelines while BPR engineers provided the skills that got the job done. I came to realize that we must work with road- and bridge-building departments rather than against them. While transportation agencies have the resources for creating great atrocities, these same resources can be directed for doing good. This potential is demonstrated by HAER's Roads and Bridges Program, which is supported by the Federal Highway Administration and state agencies. Of equal importance is the "Enhancements Program," mandated by the Intermodal Surface Transportation and Efficiency Act, where three percent of the federal highway funds allocated to the states must be used for enhancements such as historic bridge rehabilitation, railways, and roadside landscaping. This has been the single greatest source of historic preservation funding since the tax incentives program for historic building rehabilitation. However, the act expired in 1997. Industrial archaeologists must join the preservationists and environmental groups that are working to ensure that enhancement funding is continued in new surface transportation legislation.

8. James Krohe, "You Call This a National Park," *Planning* (August 1990): p. 4.

9. During the 1970s, HAER produced award-winning documentary films on two "anachronistic industries" in cooperation with the Park Service's audiovisual unit at Harpers Ferry. Still operating using turn-of-the-century technology were the Bretz coke ovens and Seneca Glass, manufacturers of fine lead-crystal glass and stemware, in West Virginia. Film and video remain the best documentation techniques for those industries retaining process, people, setting, and motion.

10. Beginning with the third TICCIH conference hosted by Sweden in 1978, national reports were prepared by participating countries that permit the comparison of the industrial heritage priorities of the respective nations. See Dianne Newell and Robert M. Vogel, "A North American Report," *The Industrial Heritage Transactions 1: National Reports, the Third International Conference on the Conservation of Industrial Monuments* (Sweden: May 30–June 5, 1978), 93–108; Eric DeLony, "L'archéologie industrielle aux Etats-Unis 1978–1981," *ICCIH 81, Volume 1, Rapports Nationaux 1978–1981, 4ᵉ Conférence Internationale pour L'étude et la Mise en Valeur du Patrimoine Industriel, CILAC* (Paris, 1981), 57–68; Eric DeLony, "Industrial Archeology in the United States 1981–1984," *Industrial Heritage '84 National Reports, Volume 1, the Fifth International Conference on the Conservation of the Industrial Heritage, Society for Industrial Archeology* (Washington, D.C., 1984), 116–23; Eric DeLony and Helena E. Wright, "United States," *TICCIH, Industrial Heritage—Austria 1987—Transactions 1, National Reports 1984–1987*, 140–49; Stephen Victor and Eric DeLony, "United States," *Industrial Heritage '92 National Reports, the 8th International Conference of the Conservation of the Industrial Heritage, Centro de Estudios Historicos de Obras Publicas y Urbanismo* (Madrid, 1992), 209–16; Dennis Zembala, "United States," *TICCIH/CSIH '94 National Reports, the Ninth International Conference on the Conservation of Industrial Heritage, Montreal/Ottawa, Canada* (1994), 65–68.

The Industrial Heritage: A Living Memory and an Instrument of Knowledge

Since the 1960s, the United States, while conserving its rank as the foremost global industrial power, has, like all the great industrialized countries, experienced episodes of deindustrialization. One by one, these crises have affected various branches and historical centers of industrial growth: the coal mines in the Appalachian Mountains, the copper and iron deposits of Lake Superior, the cotton industry in New England, the iron and steel mills in Pennsylvania and along the Atlantic coast, the automobile factories in Detroit, and the port facilities in Buffalo and New York City. The resulting economic and geographical shifts, social problems, and fossilization of entire landscapes have had a strong effect on public opinion. At the local level, the public has experienced a disintegration of a way of life that once seemed as unshakable as the country's industrial power.

Of the many reactions to deindustrialization, at least one has made it possible to protect certain traces of the earlier phases of industrialization: a personal fondness for technological culture, linked to some expertise, machine, or product, as well as a collective pride in the accomplishments of technology, science, and business ingenuity. A pride, in short, in American success at its most spectacular, pride in having led the way in the realm of material civilization. Hence, monuments of American industry that had fallen into obsolescence have become part of the heritage of a nation working to find its identity through its accomplishments, through the conquest of its territory and the achievement of its independence. American industry now has its landmarks, its historic districts, and its parks. Eric DeLony's foreword, in some sense a career retrospective, has told of the methods and successes, but also the limitations and difficulties, of transforming the traces of industry into a "heritage."

Despite a certain number of losses, the industrial heritage of the United States remains extraordinarily rich, perhaps even more so than that of Great Britain, which fancies itself the matrix of modern industrialization. Knowledge of this heritage represents an indispensable mode of approaching the history of

Sloss Furnaces in Birmingham, Alabama. The base of blast furnace No. 2, seen from the tapping shop.

American industrial growth. The exhaustive inventory of the pieces that compose this "outdoor museum," distributed among the fifty states, is far from complete. Nevertheless, in this book I will attempt to present the main themes of this heritage, using an approach that, rather than offer a simplified catalog of sites, will demonstrate how these sites constitute a valuable introduction to the history of a continent's industrialization. To that end, I have organized the book both chronologically and thematically.

First of all, I distinguish two major phases within the nearly four centuries of settlement of the territory: from the Revolutionary War to the Civil War, a phase of European-style industrialization that was characterized by the predominance of the New England states and by strong similarities between the Old and New Worlds from the vantage point of technology and the organization of work; and from the end of the Civil War until World War II, a phase of American-style industrialization that was marked by the rise of industrial giants. Several major factors contributed to the American industrial phenomenon: the wealth of resources, the dimensions of the market, the financial power of the entrepreneur class, and innovations in technology and methods of production.

In the era from World War II to the present, the growth of industrial wastelands has resulted from the deindustrialization affecting the large industrial centers—previously unparalleled in their power—while economic recovery and the migration of industries have favored both innovative sectors of production and regions that had remained marginal in the earlier waves of industrialization. The United States has entered a period of reflection on the possibilities and modalities of protection, rehabilitation, and reuse of what is now called the "industrial heritage."

Secondly, I propose a thematic analysis of the material heritage of industry, of its architectural and technical aspects, and of the way it has been inserted into the environment. That analysis highlights a certain number of traits that characterize American industrialization in particular.

The United States is a country whose conquest, settlement, and development were premised on the creation of adequate

Above: *Great Falls in Paterson, New Jersey. This spectacular waterfall was already a tourist attraction in the colonial period. The plan for the city was first commissioned from Pierre-Charles L'Enfant, who had designed the plan for Washington, D.C., and was finally executed in a less ambitious manner by Peter Colot. In 1912–14, the Society for Useful Manufactures installed a hydroelectric plant at the falls. It was closed in 1969, at a time when oil was inexpensive, but it was modernized and put back in operation in 1987.*

Left: *The Columbus Manufacturing Company, an imposing 1899 factory on the Chattahoochee River in Columbus, Georgia.*

Opposite: *The top of blast furnace C at the Bethlehem factories.*

The copper-ore processing factory of the Kennecott Copper Corporation in Alaska. The ore was extracted from the mountains more than three thousand feet above the factory. All the machinery on the interior of the building has been kept intact.

means of communication. Bridges, canals, railroads, and ports constituted a formidable set of tools, for which Americans today feel a particular affection. These structures were (and still are) the product of ingenuity, coupled with a vast reservoir of natural resources, whose exploitation implemented extraordinary technological methods but also has left deep marks on the landscape.

Industrial development was accompanied by a parallel evolution in the modes of construction. American historians of art and architecture now acknowledge the exceptional richness of industrial architecture, which is original in its forms and often pioneering in its use of materials. All these themes, all these eras have inspired painters and photographers. The presence of an aesthetic view of industry, in a book devoted to the presentation of the industrial heritage, offers another perspective and a different understanding of the cultural values of industrialization in the United States. Many exhibitions have already taken as their theme the capturing, through the painter's eye, of industry's impact on nature—an object of veneration on a continent that perceived itself as new, even if it was not truly so. At present, it is photographers who increasingly apprehend the heritage in peril, from Sandy Noyes, working on the landscapes of New England, to Joseph Elliott, performing a postmortem on Bethlehem Steel.

This book, though not an official publication of the Historic American Engineering Record, nevertheless originated in an exhibition held in 1997 at the living museum of Le Creusot—Montceau-les-Mines, with the kind and indispensable cooperation of Eric DeLony.

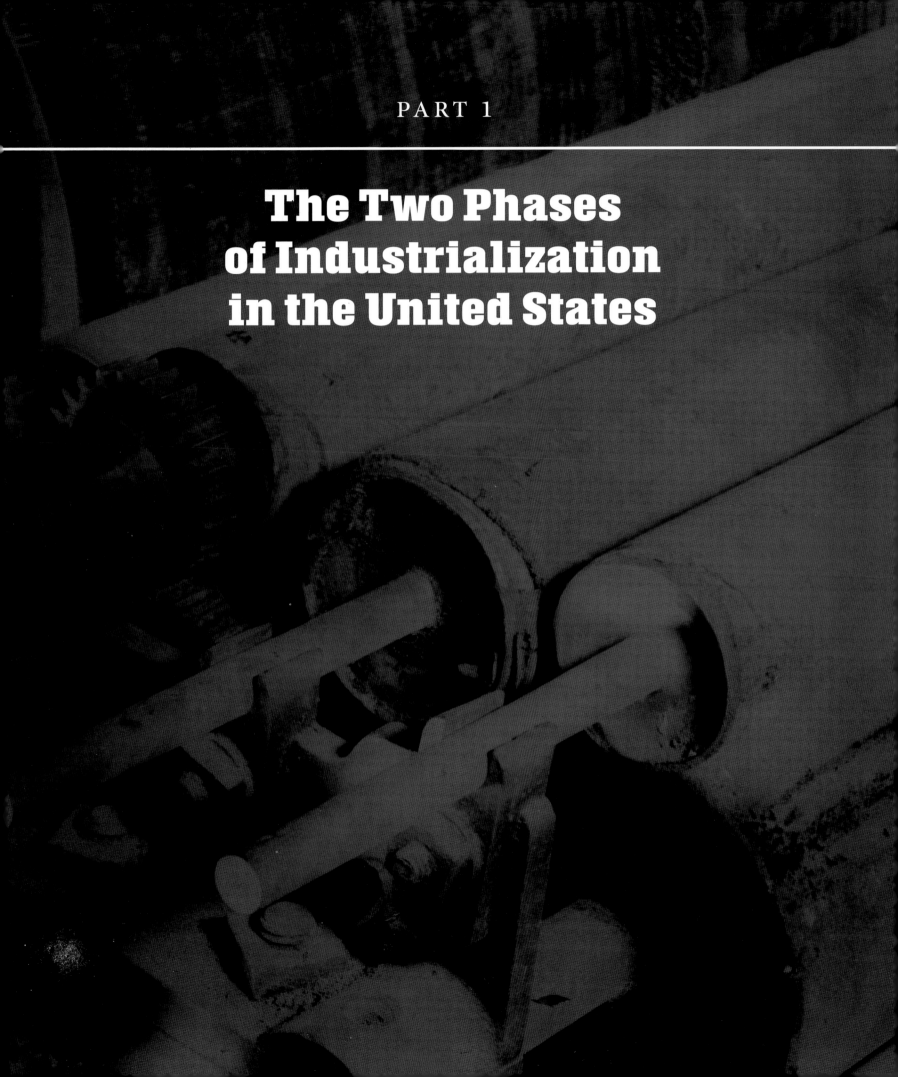

PART 1

The Two Phases of Industrialization in the United States

A "European-style" Industrialization: New England from Independence to the Civil War

The settlers who arrived in America in the seventeenth and eighteenth centuries came from the British Isles, the Netherlands, the Germanic countries, and France, bringing with them the technologies of Europe. However, until 1783, consistent with the general policy of the European nations of the time, the English colonial government imposed all sorts of limits on the development of industry in America. That in part explains the settlers' enthusiasm, as soon as independence was achieved, for developing an autonomous industrial economy and rivaling the technical prowess of their former rulers. In that regard America was akin to France, a country that was equally anxious to make up for lost time in relation to England, then the paragon of technological innovation. In addition, in the first decades following independence, the Americans showed great interest in the scientific and technological assets that France possessed, which it disseminated through its universities and the engineers they trained.

During the first half of the nineteenth century, the history of industrial development unfolded along largely similar lines in the United States and Europe. On both sides of the Atlantic, the same mills and forges could be found, the same momentous automation of the textile industry occurred, and the same industrial plants cropped up along waterways because of the predominant use of water power. The great divergence between the mode and pace of American and European growth, the era of astounding differences in scale, was yet to come. The parallels with Europe were not merely technological, but also social, given the emergence of workers' housing close to production sites, which soon gave birth to company towns and even cities, both here and abroad.

Nevertheless, the industrialization of the United States immediately conformed to the country's specific conditions: an extraordinarily forested land, endowed with hundreds of thousands of waterways, of diverse and ever-present mining resources,

Overleaf: *A detail of the cylinder cogwheels from a nineteenth-century wool-carding machine in the Watkins Glen Mill Museum in Lawson, Missouri.*

Opposite: *A discharge canal for the water returned to the Merrimack River in Lowell, Massachusetts.*

and subject to the hurdles posed by great distances. Well before tackling foreign markets, American industry found itself facing a tremendous demand associated with the claiming of the territory: the demand by a pioneer economy for sharp tools, plows, and receptacles of every kind.

METALLURGY, THE PIONEERS' HERITAGE

The New World offered all the natural resources necessary for the production of iron: ancient forests for the manufacture of charcoal; oyster shells in abundance along the coast (and limestone in the country's interior) for flux; generous rivers to provide energy for the furnaces, bellows, and hammers; and finally, rich deposits of iron ore. The most favorable locations turned out to be zones of contact between the coastal plain and the Piedmont Region, where the fall line offered the maximum power near pockets of ore.

One of the highlights of American industrial heritage is the site of Saugus, near Lynn, north of Boston. It was undoubtedly the site of the second attempt to manufacture iron in colonial America. The first, very short-lived effort had occurred in 1621–22 in Falling Creek, Virginia: an Indian insurrection put an end to it almost immediately.

In Saugus itself, the furnace and the forge were in operation only from 1652 to 1676. The business began in response to the dearth of metal products that were sorely needed by the few tens of thousands of Puritans who had settled Massachusetts since 1630. In the 1950s, the site was excavated, and the American Iron and Steel Institute decided to rebuild it on the basis of original documents. Although the Saugus site lacks authenticity, the reconstitution of the setting and of the technical process has made it one of the first tourist spots devoted to industrial heritage, concerned with making palpable and intelligible the origins of a technological culture and the memory of a people's first attempts at autonomy.

It was not until the eighteenth century that American metallurgy began rapidly to expand, particularly in Pennsylvania, where its principal center would be located for 250 years. West of Philadelphia, the preserved Hopewell Furnace is now a demonstration site for the technology of the old steel industry, built in a lasting manner on the use of charcoal. In fact, the manufacture of charcoal led to the development of a whole area of expertise, whose transmission always relied much more on direct apprenticeship under master colliers than on books. It was, in fact, a delicate product, requiring great precision in the cooking time and temperature of the wood, whose friability demanded great caution during transport and the loading of the furnaces.

From 1650 to 1750, the iron and steel industry extended up and down the Eastern seaboard, but also penetrated the interior of the Appalachian Mountains before reaching the Northwest Territories after 1789, and the Mississippi Valley in the late 1830s. The wood-powered iron and steel industry, which greatly increased the number of its sites after American independence, left behind several dozen furnaces. Their respective state of preservation is directly related to the architectural quality of their masonry.

One notable example is the furnace of Richmond, in the Berkshires in western Massachusetts, which was in operation between 1829 and 1923. It produced high-quality cast iron, which was used during the Civil War to manufacture cannons for the artillery and navy, and, until after World War I, to make train wheels and certain parts of automobile engines.

Maryland was not only the northernmost of the slave states, and a rural region long associated with tobacco wealth, it was also the site, beginning in the first decades of the eighteenth century, of many furnaces and forges. Their remains are the object of a particularly attentive historical inquiry, for they have taken on a dual patriotic significance: for having provided settlers with the nails and tools indispensable for the construction of houses and the development of their land; and for having been instrumental in the struggle for independence, thanks to their conversion into cannon and bullet foundries during the two wars waged against the British (in 1776–83, and again in 1812–14). The masters of American forges were, in fact, among the most fervent defenders of the revolution; independence emancipated them from the constraints of a ruling government bent on restricting them to the manufacture of cast iron, and reserving for itself the colonial market in finished products.

In Catoctin, in Frederick County, on the eastern slope of the Appalachian Mountains, as many as three furnaces were active between 1774 and 1892. In particular, they supplied Fort McHenry during the War of 1812, which protected the port of Baltimore when the entire Chesapeake Bay was vulnerable to British attacks. The business's founder, Thomas Johnson, was one of the leaders of the American Revolution, and was later governor of Maryland. The rectangular blast furnace, built in 1853, ran on charcoal but was fed by cold-air bellows driven by steam power.

In Nassawango, near Snow Hill, on Maryland's Eastern Shore (between Chesapeake Bay and the Atlantic Ocean), a large furnace operated, but for less than two decades (1830–47), as a result of a miscalculation of the extent and quality of the local iron-ore reserves. It is still in a remarkable state of preservation and attests to the American capacity for innovation at that time. Located near Nassawango Creek, a tributary of the Pocomoke River, it exploited the abundant wood of a nearby forest and pockets of ore similar to those that had made the Saugus forge possible. The existence of that ore was noted by a resident of Philadelphia as early as 1788; in fact, archaeological excavations conducted in the early 1970s showed that the presence of iron had not escaped the attention of Native Americans, who mined it between 750 and 250 B.C., a fact that gives this site a particularly impressive historical weight. The funerary objects found there also show that Native Americans participated in long-distance copper trade (from the Great Lakes region to Ohio and the Atlantic shore). The nozzles hanging above the furnace indicate that, in about 1835, Nassawango was one of the first furnaces in the United States—perhaps even the very first—to adopt the revolutionary British technique of blowing blasts of hot air, perfected just before 1830. The blast furnace was filled with alternating layers of charcoal, ore, and oyster shells used as flux. The resulting cast iron was sent to Baltimore and Philadelphia.

WATER MILLS, THE INFRASTRUCTURE FOR THE FIRST PHASE OF INDUSTRIALIZATION

The production of cast iron assumed a particular importance and urgency when the demand for this product was stimulated by the settlers' need for tools, and sometimes for weapons to defend the territory. But, beyond that, a whole movement, still modest in its capacities, was compelled to mobilize industry around water power. In the original thirteen colonies, the eighteenth century saw a proliferation of mills, particularly on the more modest waterways, provided the water was swift. Fitting them out, in fact, did not pose insurmountable technological problems. As in Europe, these mills had multiple uses: flour mills, oil mills, paper mills, metalworking mills, and so on. Later, they were converted into the first textile factories of the Industrial Revolution.

John D. Rockefeller Jr. can be credited with encouraging the creation, in 1951, of a network of museums known as The Historic Hudson Valley. One of its key components is Phillipsburg Manor in Tarrytown, a large suburb north of New York City, along a small river, the Pocantico. This site began with a mill in about 1650, belonging to the Dutchman Frederick Flypse (or Philipse), and was established as a manor shortly thereafter. The parts visible today are the result of the restoration and reconstruction, on the basis of eighteenth-century documents, of a mixed (agricultural, industrial, and commercial) operation. The mill shipped its flour to Manhattan, taking advantage of its position on a major route used by travelers and traders. As in Saugus, the mill's technical system has been restored with especially meticulous care.

In the late eighteenth century, the milling trade participated in its own way in the beginnings of the Industrial Revolution by accomplishing a true technological leap forward, thanks to Oliver Evans of Philadelphia. His book, entitled *The Young Millwright and Miller's Guide,* which he published with Thomas Ellicott in 1795, was for decades the bible of American builders of mills and hydraulic engines; it went through fifteen editions. The industrial archaeologists of Philadelphia have recognized his role by giving his name to their local chapter. In fact, in 1787 Evans had invented the modern mill, a multistory building where the processing of grain occurs from top to bottom, considerably increasing the mill's productivity. By the mere force of gravity, the cereal, hoisted by winch to the top of the building, descended to

the level of the millstones, then to that of the sifting machines, and finally to the ground floor, where the flour was put in sacks and sent off. Subsequently, this system contributed to the perfecting of grain-elevator technology and even to the early technology of automobile assembly.

The Evans system, rapidly imitated in Europe, was enthusiastically adopted in the United States by millers large and small, leading to a boom in mill construction in Pennsylvania, Delaware, Maryland, and Virginia. By about 1820, the Baltimore region was literally overequipped: two hundred mills were operating within a seven-mile radius of that port city. The lasting prosperity produced by the early momentum of the Industrial Revolution was so great that, for a long time, millers rejected the idea of using steam power—and of having to pay for wood and coal to produce it. Shortly thereafter, they also resisted abandoning the millstones, which certain mills operated by the dozens in the nineteenth century, in favor of the Hungarian method of grinding, that is, of gradually extracting the flour by passing the grain several times between rollers. The notion of "free" hydraulic power, however, may have been merely an illusion: the cost of maintaining the system was high, whether for the repair or the modernization of the wheels and transmission systems, or for the maintenance of dikes and canals. Americans adopted the Hungarian method only belatedly, in about 1880. In 1882, the Gambrill Mill in Baltimore was fitted with cylinders and became the largest establishment of its kind in the eastern United States.

In the end, a whole style of polymorphic industrialization was perpetuated, with earlier methods overlapping and even coexisting with more modern forms of production. It was embodied in the small or medium-sized establishments, whose remains can still be seen in many river valleys in the eastern United States. Thus, hydraulic power supported the development of a large paper industry in upstate New York, a state whose rapid demographic and economic growth in the nineteenth century made it an enormous consumer of paper and cardboard of all types. In the Connecticut River valley, between Springfield and Hartford, hydraulic power supported the development of an extraordinary range of manufactured products, from textiles and paper to

Top: *A blooming mill (the predecessor to the flatting mill) in Saugus, Massachusetts. On this site, about one third of the wrought iron was processed to satisfy the demand for iron sheets and rods. The latter were used to manufacture nails, or they were sent out in bundles. The disks used to cut the rolled sheets to the desired width are shown here. Financing for the reconstruction of the Saugus site (reopened in 1954) was provided primarily by the American Iron and Steel Institute.*

Bottom: *The blast furnace in Richmond, Massachusetts. Note the beautiful arc of molten iron, from the last charcoal blast furnace used in the United States (1829–1923). In 1926, demolition began on the buildings of the Richmond Iron Works to salvage the wood from the frame, but, on the whole, the masonry was not touched. This arch, for example, has remained intact. In the 1980s, preliminary studies of the site were undertaken, and, between 1992 and 1994, the same site was the subject of systematic surveys.*

Above: *The forge in Saugus, Massachusetts, with its system of water supply pipes and its two hydraulic driving wheels. The water came from a dam located upstream. Pipelines distributed it to the wheels, which drove the forge's large hammer. The three smokestacks vent the fires that reheat the pig iron from the blast furnace, keeping the iron malleable enough to be forged and turned into iron bars.*

Left: *From left to right: the forge, the blooming mill, and the loading port on the Saugus River. The river, navigable at high tide, was used to transport the wrought-iron products to Lynn and Boston via two or three small boats belonging to the company. The forge was sited in a marshy environment, whose peat bogs contained the iron ore it was processing.*

Left: *The blast furnace in Catoctin, Maryland, dating from the early nineteenth century, and the forge shop.*

Below: *The opening that allows the molten iron to flow from the blast furnace.*

Top: *The blast furnace (about 1840) in Nassawango, Maryland, and its loading ramp.*

Bottom: *The Methodist chapel in the workers' town of Nassawango—known as Furnace Town or Furnaceville—had been reduced to ruins, but it is now being restored, thanks to the efforts of a local foundation.*

weapons and other products of precision mechanics. The development of the Housatonic River valley, on the border of Connecticut and New York, is described in remarkable terms by Judith A. McGaw in her *Most Wonderful Machine: Mechanization and Social Change in Berkshire Paper Making, 1801–1885*. And finally, in the Hudson River valley, for a century and a half, paper mills were among the leading industries. Large establishments still attest to this legacy: the Mohawk Paper Mills in Cohoes (1917) and Albany International in Troy (1901), which remains the largest global manufacturer of felt made from wool or synthetic fibers. Such examples allow us to appreciate the importance of the first phase of industrialization, and the use of the renewable energy source of water, in the long-term organization of the country's industrial geography.

An equally remarkable example is provided by the narrow, sloping valleys that converge near the port of Baltimore. Beginning in the late 1760s, the Patapsco Valley south of the city had attracted the attention of the three Ellicott brothers, Quakers from Pennsylvania seeking their fortune in Maryland. Their first mill produced plaster designed to improve floors. A second, then a third mill produced flour, which the brothers soon exported via Baltimore. In about 1800, these mills were considered the largest and most sophisticated in the region. In the early nineteenth century, a sawmill, an oil works, a rolling mill, and a nail manufacture were developed. Another family created a paper mill and a cotton factory. Two miles downstream, in Thistle, a company town, with about thirty houses around a cotton-print factory, appeared in about 1824. In 1830, the Ellicott City train station became the terminus for the first section of the railway line (about twelve-and-a-half miles long) to be built by the Baltimore and Ohio Railroad, which had chosen to use that corridor to begin to penetrate the Appalachian Mountains. Somewhat later, Edward Weber, a Baltimore lithographer, took on the task of drawing illustrations of the factories in Ellicott City, which became quite famous as a result.

In contrast, the Johns Falls River Valley, today enclosed within the Baltimore metropolitan area, and whose existence the city residents seem to have almost forgotten, constitutes a true industrial park of several hundred acres. Beginning in 1719, the waterfalls were used for a flour mill; the Rockland Grist Mill and the houses surrounding it, dating from the late eighteenth century, are reminders of this era. The valley became one of the most exploited hydraulic sites in Maryland in the mid-nineteenth century: twenty-three mills, foundries, and various manufactures made it the state's largest industrial concentration. A set of buildings, all associated with the textile industry, stand today as witnesses connecting the urban culture of Baltimore to 250 years of industrialization along the water.

THE ALLIANCE OF TEXTILES AND HYDRAULIC POWER

The most explicit factor in the industrial growth along America's waterways was the textile industry, wool and cotton for the most part. After putting the falls and the buildings of the traditional mills to a new use, after two or three decades the textile industry moved its shops to sites of their own, where the adoption of unprecedented technological solutions allowed the industry to respond to the very rapid growth of the domestic market. It was the pressure of that market, as well as military needs and political circumstances, that forced the industry to change its scale.

The first factories, small in size, exploited waterfalls with relatively little power. The site of Slater Mill, in Pawtucket, Rhode Island, is as significant as that of Saugus, evoking the beginnings of English-style mechanization in the early American republic: it stands as the birthplace of industrialization in the United States. It is there that Samuel Slater, born in Belper, England, in 1768, came to settle in 1789, bringing with him the British cotton technology of the period. He offered to form a company with Smith Brown and William Almy, the nephew and son-in-law, respectively, of Moses Brown, a Providence merchant who, beginning in 1787, had attempted in vain to manufacture a cotton thread resistant enough to fit out a loom. Slater had no difficulty building, on site and with the means available, the first cotton-spinning machines, modeled on Arkwright's water frame—to the great dismay of the English, who were making every effort to prevent their technology and technicians from leaving for the former colonies or for other countries of the Old World. These machines equipped the first successful cotton mills in the United States. In 1792, the partners erected a dam on the falls of Blackstone River in Pawtucket, slightly north of Providence; in 1793, the factory itself was built—it still survives in the center of the city of Pawtucket. A modest establishment, in 1820 the mill employed only about thirteen men, five women, and fifty-two children.

These seminal events can be linked to what was happening in the early years of the nineteenth century in Harrisville, in the Monadnock region at the southwestern tip of New Hampshire, which is rich in flowing water and stagnant ponds. There, in about 1804, recently arrived settlers—landowners or local artisans—successfully began operating wool-carding machines driven by hydraulic power. This type of machine had been designed by trial and error in the 1790s in various places in New England; the American Museum of Textile History, in Lowell, Massachusetts, has on display a few superb models, with frames made completely of wood. It did not take long before the promoters, Harris and Twitchell, had success, stimulated by the effects of the War of 1812. Harrisville shut down all operations in 1970, but its factories and company town were immediately protected through the creation of a historic district. Similarly, in Andover, Massachusetts, the Cochichewick Falls (a seventy-two-foot drop) were used by the wool industry beginning in 1802; today, the city preserves the buildings of the Davis & Furber textile machine company (1836–1982), surrounded by its workers' housing. The oldest hydraulic spinning mill in Maryland, Mount Washington Mill on the Johns Falls River in Baltimore, was created in 1809 to supply thread to the home weavers of cotton duck, an industry stimulated by the War of 1812 and the break in commercial ties with England.

Also in 1812, this same conflict—the second war of independence—occasioned the creation in Waltham, on the Charles River (now in the Boston metropolitan area), of a business bearing the marks of a more organized form of capitalism. Francis Cabot Lowell, who came from a family of major Boston wholesalers whose business was hobbled by British competition, had visited Great Britain and returned with the conviction that the future lay in the mechanization of the spinning and weaving of cotton. With a few partners, he founded the Boston Manufacturing Company, hired the services of the engineer Paul Moody, a machine builder and an inventor, and entrusted him with the task of building the equipment that could not be imported from England. That was the beginning of the Waltham factory, created as a joint-stock company. It was the second phase in the establishment of an American textile industry, an industrial branch enjoying real autonomy.

Thus, the beginnings of the industrialization of textiles in New England do not date from the years 1821–22, which witnessed the start of the construction of the famous hydraulic system of Lowell, but rather from a generation earlier. As symbolic as that event may appear in retrospect, it does not in any way constitute an absolute historical origin. During the previous ten or twenty years, a number of textile businesses of modest size had begun to occupy sites at modest waterfalls, especially the tributaries of the Merrimack. That first generation, whose scale, to be sure, did not approach that of Lowell, nevertheless performed the first experiments in the mechanization of cotton- and wool-working.

In the 1820s, the Bostonian capitalists repeated the Waltham experiment in Dover, New Hampshire, where they created two industrial complexes (for spinning, weaving, and printing), as well as the first boarding houses for young female workers and a commercial district. Unfortunately, that small town has suffered a lot of demolition as a result of urban renewal policy.

THE RISE IN THE SCALE OF POWER

From the 1820s to the 1840s, a change of scale marked the entry of the eastern United States into the ranks of the great industrial powers. This was made possible thanks to a new technology, the fruit of a knowledge of engineering, that allowed for the diversion of the waters of much more powerful rivers, such as the Merrimack and the Connecticut, which rushed down from the eastern slope of the Appalachian Mountains toward the Atlantic Ocean. These rivers reached the coastal plain via a series of closely spaced falls, sometimes with a sharp drop, whose accumulated power

Left: *At Philipsburg Manor in Tarrrytown, New York, the bridge on the dam of the mill's reservoir pond, with the dealer's house in the background.*

Top: *Between the mill and the cowshed stands the nineteenth-century house of the mill's founder, a dealer of Dutch origin. It is currently open to the public as a house museum.*

Above: *The water supply pipe and the mill wheel.*

Above: *Aerial view of the site of Slater Mill in Pawtucket, Rhode Island, on the Blackstone River. Opened as a museum in 1955, it displays a collection of textile machines.*

Opposite, upper and lower right: *A nineteenth-century woolen mill in Harrisville, New Hampshire. The building's ecclesiastical appearance stems from the presence of a clock tower at the back of the shop.*

Opposite, lower left: *A dam on the Blackstone River, upstream from Slater Mill.*

made it possible to create high-density industrial areas. Louis C. Hunter, an expert on the history of technology in the United States and the author of a comprehensive survey in three volumes (*History of Industrial Power in the United States, 1750–1830*), in 1979 published the first volume under the title *Waterpower in the Century of Steam*. The book summarizes an essential chapter of the history of American industrial power, that is, a major industry's decisive and long-lasting recourse to water power, which was established on a scale unparalleled in the rest of the contemporary world, and with an efficiency equal, if not superior, to steam power. In the early nineteenth century, American technology remained under the British influence. The vertical water wheels, first made of wood, then of iron—the latter material gave them greater longevity and power—were inspired by methods perfected in the middle of the previous century by English engineers. The best-performing wheel was called a *side* or *breast* wheel, terms referring to the part of the wheel struck by the water—skillfully directed by the intake system—which then communicated its power to it. Wheels of this type, built in the United States until about 1850, sometimes reached three hundred horsepower, a far higher force than that produced by European wheels.

The Fourneyron or Jonval models of turbines, of French origin, were introduced into the United States in the 1840s and became widespread in the 1850s and 1860s in the cotton industry of New England and the Central Atlantic states. Subsequently, new turbines drawing on specifically American technology took root; they arose from a preference for a different mode of introducing the water into the generator, a technique gradually perfected by the chief engineer at the Locks and Canals Company of Lowell, and by a few others. These turbines achieved very high effective yields, adapted to every demand and every flow, and were very rustic in their construction and simple to manufacture. Because they were mass-produced, they were inexpensive. Still later (in the early 1880s), the Pelton turbine, called the *tangential injection* turbine, was perfected, allowing the introduction of water from high falls and under very high pressure, thus corresponding to the requirements of mining operations in the Rocky Mountains, which needed high-performance extraction machines

and pumps. Then, with the aid of steel metallurgy (in the absence of which these engines would not have been built), hydraulic energy accompanied industrial growth in the United States into the period of westward expansion.

PATERSON AND LOWELL: THE BIRTH OF A TECHNOLOGICAL MODEL

The first example of a more complete domestication of hydraulic power dates from the industrial planning operation carried out in Paterson, New Jersey. The statue of Alexander Hamilton, founder of the city, still stands near Great Falls (an eighty-two-foot drop). Hamilton, an aide-de-camp and secretary to General George Washington, had spent time in the region during the Revolutionary War and sensed the extraordinary industrial potential of the site. As a result, he became the defender of an independent and protected national industry. The Society for Establishing Useful Manufactures, of which he was a founder, devised a plan for a rational use of hydraulic power by connecting a series of factories along a network of canals that would channel the waters of the Passaic River. Hamilton was thus an important catalyst in the first centrally planned industrial city in American history.

Paterson devoted itself to the cotton industry and to the manufacture of textile equipment, until the Civil War and the resulting "cotton famine" led to the conversion of its machine works. Thomas Rogers, formerly a builder of textile machines, began production of locomotives for the Union troops, then for the conquest of the West, and finally for the Trans-Siberian Railway. Another consequence of the war was the conversion to silk manufacturing, an industry for which Paterson became, in 1870, the foremost center in the United States.

The system of reducing hydraulic power via a network of channels feeding a factory district was carried out successfully in Lowell, Massachusetts, today considered the cradle of industrialization in the United States. This success was due to the judicious investment on the part of a group of Bostonian capitalists—among them Francis Cabot Lowell, the city's namesake—and the talents of the engineer Kirk Boott, trained in England at the

Royal Military Academy Sandhurst. But, in reality, Lowell's triumph was due to the Merrimack, a river whose characteristics warrant consideration. Regular in its flow, adequate even in the dry season, it runs in an area whose topography forms vast pool reservoirs. Because the river lies in a rocky bed and flows between steep banks, the dams could be solidly anchored. The river's size and power, however, exceeded the capacities of public-works engineering of the colonial period and the early years of the republic; the oldest factories were established on more modest tributaries. The impressive power of Pawtucket Falls (a thirty-three-foot drop), upstream from Lowell, thus remained unexploited, while the riverside farmers captured only a fraction of the river's force with the aid of small spur dams that did not require much capital or expertise.

One canal, the Middlesex, had been built to allow trading ships to bypass Pawtucket Falls. In 1796, a company called The Proprietors of Locks and Canals decided to compete with the Middlesex by building the Pawtucket Canal. It was a commercial failure, but its construction opened the way for its reuse in 1822 as a power canal feeding the first large factory in Lowell, the Merrimack Manufacturing Company.

From 1822 to 1847, a series of power canals were installed, supplying some ten thousand horsepower. The partners in the Boston Manufacturing Company, having identified the potential of Merrimack Falls and the increase in profit they could expect from it, purchased the canal without encountering any resistance from the latter's shareholders, who were unaware of the boon hydraulic energy represented. They had no more difficulty taking the adjacent lands away from farmers, who were unable to make enough from farming to compete with the value their properties were likely to acquire. The operations and installations that followed were conducted by Kirk Boott and led to the formation of new companies, with shareholders who often participated in several businesses at a time: Hamilton (1825), Appleton (1828), Middlesex (1830), Suffolk & Tremont (1832), Lawrence (1833), Boott (1835), and Massachusetts (1840). Today the network of power canals, ten miles long, is practically intact. There, hydraulic power was used alongside steam well into the twentieth century.

Of all the factories that sprouted up in Lowell throughout the nineteenth century, admirers of American industrial heritage give a special place to the Boott Mills (named in tribute to the engineer who endowed Lowell industry with the energy that drove it). Six factories were built between 1835 and 1845, between the Merrimack and the Eastern Canal (opened in 1835–36 over a length of twenty-three hundred feet), to which several other buildings were added in the 1860s. In addition to a nephew and a son-in-law of the founder Lowell, the shareholders were Abbot Lawrence (later involved in two businesses in the city that bears his name) and Appleton (also a Hamilton shareholder). There was nothing particularly rational, in terms of distribution and the organization of work, about the burgeoning of this business, which manufactured both cotton and wool. But its long existence conveys in a remarkable way the phases of power and automation in the textile industry. The hydraulic power available to the factories was first increased by the creation of the Northern Canal in about 1845. The vertical (breast) wheels were later replaced by powerful turbines, several of which survive: two Swain turbines from 1874–75, with a very high yield (eighty-six percent), produced up to three and four hundred horsepower. It was only in 1885 that a twenty-four hundred horsepower steam generator was installed; but other models of turbines (Allis-Chalmers, Leffels) were fitted out in the 1920s and 1940s.

In the beginning, Lowell's mills chose to produce a limited range of rather coarse fabrics, which required little skill to manufacture. The manager recruited a female labor force from within a narrow radius, and these women were trained by men. By 1850, Lowell had become the second-largest city in Massachusetts, after Boston. From 1850 to 1920, immigration from Quebec and Europe increased its population to one hundred thousand, eighty percent of which had been born abroad. Lowell's decline began in 1920, when the cotton industry migrated to the South. Many former factories and workers' rowhouses were destroyed at that time.

THE SUCCESS OF THE MODEL IN NEW ENGLAND

The industrial success of Lowell led to the creation of the city of Lawrence, seven miles downstream on the Merrimack. There, the

Two buildings of Mount Washington Mill in the Johns Falls Valley in Baltimore, Maryland.

Top: *A superb granite plant from 1809;*

Bottom: *a twentieth-century brick shop.*

Above: *Paterson, New Jersey, was the first American city to have a system for distributing hydraulic power by a network of canals.*

Left: *The late-nineteenth-century American Thread Mill on the Willimantic River in Connecticut is an eloquent tribute to the use of hydraulic power for more than one hundred years by the large New England textile mills. A spinning mill was located on this site by 1825; another replaced it in 1854. With the invention of the sewing machine, a number of buildings were added to the site.*

Lowell, Massachusetts.

Left: *The gatehouse (right) and the lock house (left) viewed from upstream.*

Above: *The dam on the Merrimack River at Pawtucket Falls, across from the offtake that feeds the entire canal system.*

48

Top: *Water gates take in water to feed the hydraulic engines located in a factory basement in Paterson, New Jersey.*

Above: *A vault feeds water into basement turbines in Lowell, Massachusetts.*

Right: *In Lowell, the manual control levers (screw mechanisms) of the water gates located in the gatehouse make it possible to regulate the intake of water from the Pawtucket Canal into the water distribution system. Contemporary American industrial archaeologists consider these canals more than functional necessities; they see them as an early effort to beautify American cities.*

Opposite: *Part of Amoskeag Mills in Manchester, New Hampshire, before the canal was filled in.*

Above: *The gatehouse overseeing the offtake of the Mohawk River in Cohoes, New York.*

Right: *The gatehouse in front of the water distribution system in Augusta, Georgia.*

hydraulic system was fitted out in 1845–48 by Essex Company, the owner of all the property on which the city was to be built, and by its chief engineer, Charles Storrow. The influence of the most recent designs by French hydraulic engineers could be seen in the layout, slope, and profile of the canal. Between 1880 and 1920, Lawrence became the largest production center of worsted wool in the world. This second major center also made use of the combined power of water and steam to run enormous factories, built in the first decade of the twentieth century, at the impetus, in particular, of the American Woollen Company. In the late nineteenth century, the Arlington Mills, created in 1834 and rebuilt in the early 1880s, used eight steam engines to run 132,000 spindles and 2,600 wool-spinning and -weaving looms, plus 100,000 spindles for spinning fine cotton thread. The Ayer Mills, another giant wool mill dating from 1910, also used steam power exclusively. But the Lawrence Manufacturing Company operated on hydraulic power for the most part (3,500 of its 6,200 horsepower), and six of its Hercules turbines from the years 1909–16 still survive. The Pemberton Mills (built in about 1860) were equipped with three turbines, dating from 1891. The Upper Pacific Mills, the property of Abbot Lawrence, operated on eighty percent water power, running 150,000 spindles, 4,600 looms, and twenty-five printing machines in about 1890 (the building, nearly 2,000 feet long and eighty feet wide, was unfortunately torn down around 1960).

Lowell industrialization was in the end only one component of a powerful industrial network in nineteenth-century New England, composed of mills for spinning and weaving cotton and wool, and hosiery factories. This network was centered along the Merrimack River, of course, but also along its tributaries, and included, in addition to Lawrence, the cities of Methuen and Amesbury downstream, and Manchester and Nashua, both in New Hampshire, upstream. Until the early twentieth century, the entire Merrimack hydrographic basin attracted businessmen and investors, and very few falls in the southern part of New Hampshire were not exploited, primarily by the textile industry. By about 1880, some nine hundred hydraulic factories were installed on the tributaries of the Merrimack, each with an average of thirty horsepower.

After Lowell, Manchester provides the most compelling evidence of the high-density areas characteristic of the American textile industry. The Amoskeag Manufacturing Company exploited the Amoskeag Falls, a fifty-two-foot drop more than 2,600 feet along the Merrimack, falls that surpassed by twenty-five percent the power of the Pawtucket River. Amoskeag Manufacturing, created in 1831, also built a dam and a dual system of power canals, which were filled in during the urban renewal operations of the early 1970s. These operations also demolished many structures soon after the New England Textile Mills Survey, which was a unique undertaking at the time in the United States and was, fortunately, able to inventory the structures. Between 1838 and 1910, Amoskeag Manufacturing constructed more than thirty buildings, of which eighteen survive. The company employed up to 15,000 workers on 670,000 spindles and 24,000 looms—a global giant.

Farther to the north, in Lewiston, Maine, landowners and holders of water rights, encouraged by Lowell's success, sought in the 1830s to take full advantage of Great Falls, on the Androscoggin River. They too created a network of canals and an industrial city. The plan was completed in the late 1840s, with the support of capital from Massachusetts and of first-rate engineers such as David Whitman, originally from Rhode Island, and nicknamed "the mill doctor," and John B. Straw, from Lowell.

THE SPREAD OF THE LOWELL SYSTEM

The Lowell model, which consisted of developing an industrial district from a system of canals diverting a waterway, won a following beyond New England, and first and foremost in Cohoes, New York, near the confluence of the Mohawk and Hudson Rivers and the junction of the Champlain and Erie Canals. The latter had been completed in 1825 and connected Albany to Buffalo. In about 1831–34, falls there were equipped with a dam feeding a system of canals. In 1826, the Cohoes Company, with 250,000 dollars in capital, was formed by New York capitalists: a cotton manufacturer from Rhode Island—none other than the brother-in-law of Samuel Slater—and Canvass White, an

Above: *Painting by Bass Otis of the Eleutherian Mills, Du Pont de Nemours's first industrial plant, in Greenville, Delaware.*

Left: *The Willimantic River in Connecticut. Rapid water in a wooded environment provided a favorable setting for the first industrial plants.*

54 engineer and canal builder and the inventor of hydraulic cement. Like Alexander Hamilton in Paterson, White dreamed of transforming Cohoes into a large industrial city. The principal landowner in the region, Van Rensselaer of Albany, supported the project by giving up, in exchange for one dollar, his water rights on the Mohawk and some land along the Hudson River. Cohoes and its large cotton factories thus merged with the neighboring cities of Albany and Troy to form the second-largest industrial region in the United States before the Civil War.

One of the first to take advantage of the canal system was Samuel Garner, the founder of the Harmony Manufacturing Company in 1837. In the late 1860s, his installations, in the opinion of the eminent British engineer Evan Leigh, represented the latest thing in American cotton technology. At the same time, his new buildings, along with a carefully constructed company town, offered the foremost example of a large-scale cotton complex outside New England.

The South, following its defeat in the Civil War, adopted the same model that had succeeded in the north. The presence of spinning and weaving mills now superseded the classic image of a region entirely devoted to a raw-cotton economy inherited from slavery. That was the case in Columbus and Augusta, both in Georgia.

Beginning in 1828, thanks to falls with a 130-foot drop over two-and-a-half miles along the Chattahoochee, Columbus was able to set up a series of flour mills, textile manufactures, and other factories along its banks; later, during the Civil War, it became the arsenal of the Confederate army. The Columbus Ironworks supplied cannons and steam engines for the war effort. The river offered the potential of 100,000 horsepower, very close to that of Pawtucket Falls in Lowell, which explains why Columbus became one of the leaders of industrialization in the South. When the Historic American Engineering Record (HAER) undertook the inventory of Columbus's industrial heritage, the factories on the banks of the river were still operating with their turbines and generators, conserving the city's industrial fabric, more than a century old, over a length of one mile. That zone became a national historic landmark in 1978.

Finally, one should not forget the case of Minneapolis, Minnesota, where the Falls of Saint Anthony and the diversion of the waters of the Mississippi served to support development of the most powerful flour-mill zone in the world, the West Side Milling District, stocked with its collection of reinforced-concrete grain elevators dating from the first third of the twentieth century. This area was declared a historic district. The Washburn Mill at its center is now a national historic landmark: this birthplace of the cylinder milling technique, dating from 1874, was rebuilt out of limestone in 1880 after an explosion, and fitted out with concrete grain elevators dating from 1908 to 1928. Unfortunately, it lost most of its old equipment as a result of fires in 1928 and then in 1991.

THE AMERICAN INDUSTRIAL LANDSCAPE TAKES SHAPE

Since the beginning of the nation, two conflicting notions of America have faced off: on the one hand, that of an agrarian society of physiocratic inspiration, defended with particular vigor by Thomas Jefferson in his *Notes on the State of Virginia* (1785), which questioned the advisability of American society setting out on the path of industrialization; and, on the other hand, that of the pro-industrialists, propounded notably by Alexander Hamilton in his *Report on Manufactures* (1790), which is strongly nationalist in tone. At issue was nothing less than the definition of the social and spiritual configuration of the new republic. Would it remain faithful to its original traditions—a society of settlers, of small landowners and artisans sustained by the virtues of family, religion, and rural communities—or would it evolve toward an English-style urbanized and industrialized society, destroying all the physical and moral benefits of maintaining its roots in the rural areas?

The traditionalists appealed to the myth of America as a sort of natural paradise, bequeathed by God to the Americans. But the proponents of vigorous industrial development, bolstered by the consequences of the War of 1812, had no difficulty tipping the balance in favor of their views, maintaining that industrialization represented a fundamental aspect of national independence, and that it was now inconceivable to continue to embrace Jefferson's declaration—"Let our workshops remain in Europe." The proponents of industrialization defended the idea that industry could be introduced with perfect harmony into the American landscape, all the while making brute nature productive. The domestication of power by the mills, the exploitation of natural resources, these assets would transform America into a land of prosperity. Machines, in bringing material progress and greater social equality, would work in the public interest. On the moral front, Lowell management made every effort to demonstrate that a young and female labor force could be employed without becoming corrupted, exploited, or cut off from their family roots.

In the first decades of the nineteenth century, the pro-industrialists were careful to explain that the use of water power (and not steam) allowed them to locate factories in the heart of primal nature—a nature that had been subjugated and improved. In addition, no one yet claimed that industry was destined to become the chief sector of productivity.

In the years 1800–20, the landscapes painted by certain American artists served these idyllic views held by the proponents of industrialization and contributed toward promoting a positive image of it. Adopting a conciliatory approach, these artists (whom art history has ignored until a relatively recent date) introduced factories into the backgrounds of primarily bucolic landscapes. One of the first illustrations was a depiction of the Pennington Mills, in a painting by Francis Guy entitled *Jones Falls Valley Looking Upstream* (1804). In 1812, John Rubens Smith painted *View of Pawtucket Bridge and Falls*. And in 1840 the painter Bass Otis depicted the Eleutherian Mills as a central motif; Eleuthère-Irénée Du Pont had built his gunpowder-manufacturing mill on the Brandywine River in 1802–04.

All the same, the reality, still perceptible today through the evidence of industrial archaeology, was undoubtedly more nuanced. The landscapes of old industry seem rather to have had two images: the first large brick factories in the English style, driven by the power of the large coastal rivers; and more modest installations, furnaces operating on charcoal until the 1860s, family milling operations, small manufactures set up along the secondary hydraulic network. Despite the presence of a certain number of smokestacks, all these elements were still in harmony with a plentiful nature of woods and water, only slightly compromised here and there by the first factories. Beyond certain similarities, however, the hydraulic plants in the mid-nineteenth century were constructed on a scale that was glaringly different from that of Old World industry, and they signaled the entry of the United States into a different age of industrial civilization. Rustic New England, mountainous and forested, was also the birthplace of steam power. In 1827, in Providence, Rhode Island, Samuel Slater, father of the cotton industry, built a steam-driven cotton mill that was supplied with Pennsylvania coal. And it was also in Providence that George H. Corliss's famous fixed steam engine originated. Patented in 1849 and mass-produced beginning in 1856, it was to equip all of America. Around the turn of the century, not far from Providence, on the other side of the Massachusetts border, Fall River was to become (in spite of its name) a major center of textile production entirely dependent on steam.

In the age of the railroad, of steel, and of coal, the New World reversed its perspective, interpreting the artificial forest of smokestacks and even the smoke streaming from them as the new symbols of its prosperity. The conciliatory ideology was abandoned by mid-century. Without hesitation, society glorified the factory, the machine, bridges and railroads, and industry as it migrated to the cities.

CHAPTER 2

The Rise of Industrial Giants: From the Civil War to World War II

During the period between the Civil War and World War II, settlement and economic growth received a tremendous boost in the United States. That boom continued to benefit the textile sector, the driving industrial force of the previous era. But it was expressed to an even greater extent in the formation of a strong metallurgical sector, stimulated as much by the enormous demands of an expanding nation as by the creation of a major military apparatus. The end of this period was characterized by the explosion of a mass industry in the form of automobile construction, which left its mark as a model of work organization.

IN THE TEXTILE INDUSTRY, THE ERA OF GIANT FACTORIES

The giant textile factories were an expression of a huge emerging market. They were vast buildings, long and narrow, four to seven stories high, which truly deserved the nickname "brick cathedrals." The term is not inaccurate in the image it evokes, as the buildings were often topped by pinnacles and had stairwells that seemed to form false buttresses on the exterior. In the United States, in the last third of the nineteenth century, there was always at any given moment a spinning or weaving business that could legitimately boast the title "the largest in the world," that could claim a record in the number of employees or a dominant position in the market for one product or another. For the last thirty years, the proliferation of these mighty edifices has raised some of the most vexing problems related to the policy of protecting the American heritage. Nevertheless, these buildings are also jewels of this heritage: solid, elegant, and relatively easy to convert, thanks to the multiple purposes to which they can be put (residences, small businesses, cultural or commercial centers, and so on).

One of the first of these audacious buildings appeared in Cohoes, New York. The development company for Mohawk Falls (a ninety-foot drop) had built a six-story power canal to exploit

The Goodyear Airdock (1929), a dirigible construction shop in Akron, Ohio.

the falls' potential. Harmony Mills, which had begun construction in 1837, used the upper levels of this system. Between 1868 and 1872, the development of this complex of cotton manufactures culminated in the construction of factory no. 3, called "Mastodon Mill." This building, eleven hundred feet long, was one of the first manifestations of the gigantic scale that characterized the textile industry in the late nineteenth and early twentieth centuries. The towers on its facade loomed over the more than nine hundred housing units built by the company, forming a company town quite different from the first boardinghouses in Lowell.

A few years later, in 1877, in Baltimore, Maryland, a new component of the manufacturing complex in the Johns Falls River Valley was built: Meadow Mill. Even though its dimensions were markedly less ambitious than those of the Cohoes mill, that four-story structure, linked to several complementary buildings erected at the same time, had similar formal characteristics. Its monumentality arose from the symmetrical structure of the facades. A dozen openings to the right and left of the massive central tower facing the city, a stairwell on the opposite side, and a mighty belfry with a pyramidal roof topped by a cupola created an impressive presence and seemed to beckon workers to the factory. The factory dominated the new company town nearby, on the other side of the river, which played an important role in the organization of the city. This monumentality was also an expression of the growth and organizational structure in that branch of industry. The Hooper dynasty—founder William, and sons Theodore, James, and Alcaeus—took the cotton-duck industry to its apogee and inaugurated a systematic company-housing policy. The preservation of these factories in their entirety, factories that have changed hands many times but have always been in operation, has made it possible to visualize a major phase of nineteenth-century industrialization.

The South, in the aftermath of its defeat in the Civil War, hastened to adopt New England's hydraulic system, its architectural models, and its company towns. (Between 1945 and 1970, to acquire the capital needed for modernization, the companies that built these towns sold housing lots to their workers.) The silhouettes of some of these factories can still be seen, standing proudly along the rivers. As early as 1877, the factory of the Enterprise Manufacturing Company, in Augusta, Georgia, made evident the fact that the construction style characteristic of the northeastern United States was spreading to the South. In an 1887 article in *Harper's Weekly,* the buildings of the Sibley Manufacturing Company (1880), also in Augusta, were described as those of a "model manufacture" of the new industrial South.

But the example of Columbus, Georgia, is even more illuminating. Columbus, a city built on the Chattahoochee River at the starting point of its navigable section, was, by virtue of its privileged locale, an entryway to the Gulf of Mexico for products manufactured in western Georgia and the Atlanta region. There, in about 1828, entrepreneurs had begun to exploit hydraulic power and, by the 1840s, several cotton mills and wool-carding manufactures lined the banks of the river. In 1865, General James Wilson's Union troops burned down Columbus's factories, but reconstruction began immediately. Hence, the Eagle Manufacturing Company of 1851 was renamed Eagle & Phenix Manufacturing Company, and it built a new factory capable of competing with Augusta, which was known as the "Lowell of the South." Beginning in 1880, the Chattahoochee was also exploited to produce hydroelectricity, and, until the 1930s, the textile and metallurgical industries continued to expand unremittingly along its banks. Today, in a time when the location of industry has become completely independent of waterways, the intact buildings of the Eagle & Phenix and Columbus Ironworks, and even those of the Empire Mills (a large flour mill operating between 1875 and 1900), have considerable historical and symbolic value.

Nevertheless, in the late nineteenth century and the first decades of the twentieth, attention turned back to New England, whose textile industry was then at its height, before the great relocation of that activity to the South beginning in 1920. It was during this period that the most impressive buildings were erected. In Lawrence, Massachusetts, the Ayer Mills provide particularly remarkable evidence, thanks to a restoration in 1960, only several years after the mills were closed in 1954. That factory had been among the first large installations in the region to operate entirely on steam. Lawrence became, between 1880 and 1920, the largest center for the production of worsted in the world, a production dominated by the American Woollen Company. The extraordinary architectural quality of the Ayer Mills can be credited to the Charles T. Main Agency of Boston. That same quality is also found in other large-scale factories built, not of brick, but of fine-quality granite. They can be found in the historic district of Fall River, Massachusetts, and in Windham, Connecticut, where the massive and imposing factory of the American Thread Company stands.

The period was marked by a boom in activity for the large industrial engineering offices, which imposed a uniform style and a standard of excellent construction on American factories. The most famous firm is still Lockwood & Greene, founded in Boston in 1832, and today located in Spartanburg, South Carolina.

The availability of the largest domestic market in the world—and one of the best protected—coupled with technological supremacy in the engineering of factories, as well as entire cities, translated into the incomparable group of textile factories that still stand in Manchester, New Hampshire, despite the fact that they ceased operation in 1938.

Named after its British counterpart, the city was a creation of Amoskeag Manufacturing Company, which, from 1837 to the early twentieth century, gradually built about thirty factories and, by the end of that period, had seventeen thousand employees—each of the factories in itself was equivalent to a manufacture of a respectable size. They were spread out over about a mile, appearing, from the Merrimack side, like a defensive wall enclosing the city. From the inside, they overlooked an enormous central courtyard used to move merchandise by water and rail. The complex was a city as much as a giant factory, entirely controlled by a business that had developed paternalism to its highest level. The labor force (immigrants for the most part, composed of French-Canadians and Irish, and later of Greeks and Poles) experienced both the benefits and the burden of that system. A book by the historian and anthropologist Tamara Hareven and the photographer Randolph Langenbach (1978) has reconstructed the factory's operations from interviews with surviving workers (both men and women) and from a remarkable photographic documentation.

THE ARRIVAL OF THE COKE-FUELED IRON AND STEEL INDUSTRY

With the second half of the nineteenth century, a new geographic division of American industry appeared, along with the birth of an entirely different form of industrial heritage. Its location was determined by that of the coal and iron ore deposits. A full range of needs, related to westward expansion and the construction of large, new infrastructures, had to be satisfied. As a result, the development of densely populated industrial centers occurred at sites where one or another of these resources was located, but even more so along the transportation waterways that joined them together and near the large urban markets and maritime ports.

As a result, an entirely new industrial landscape was created. The lands expropriated for business uses now encompassed dozens of acres. These businesses depended on immediate contact with waterways or railroads, and constructed a multiplicity of technological installations and buildings, reflecting the complexity of the manufacturing process. The manufacture of semi-finished products—metallurgy in the narrow sense—required the use of buildings that remained within the realm of large, functional architecture, but subject to new requirements or adaptable to new techniques. In contrast, the processing of raw materials—coal and metal ores—led to the intrusion on the landscape of massive instruments totally divorced from architecture: the blast furnace and the surrounding apparatus that fed it solids (coke, iron ore) or gases (forced air), or that drew off the gas produced by fusion or combustion, became the dominant components of the new industrial age. It was now possible to speak of a certain dehumanization of the workplace, as well as of a loss of the industrial apparatus's immediate intelligibility and a

dizzying growth in its size. All these circumstances have led to our current difficulties in protecting, interpreting, and reintegrating this type of heritage.

In about 1830–40, Pennsylvania began to play a central role, replacing the iron and steel industry of western Connecticut and the Adirondacks region. Many ruins from the mining and iron and steel industries continue to attest to this fact. A region with a very strong rural and agricultural heritage, Pennsylvania also became, in the second half of the nineteenth century, the industrial heart of the United States. In the eastern and western parts of the state, coal and iron mines were developed, as well as small industrial centers, large metropolises (Philadelphia, Pittsburgh), and natural transportation corridors as important as those of New York for establishing ties between the East and the Midwest.

Before 1860, the charcoal furnaces, modernized to accommodate blasts of hot air, had taken over the Schuylkill, Delaware, and Juniata valleys in the region surrounding Philadelphia, and then had become concentrated farther to the west, around Pittsburgh. The techniques for reducing iron ore and manufacturing wrought iron with the aid of charcoal were in no way archaic in the United States in the nineteenth century; in fact, they were improved in many ways in that period. In contrast, American steel remained too expensive and substandard in quality, despite the many experiments conducted by the Franklin Institute of Philadelphia. It was not until the end of the century that American steel established itself as the product of a particularly advanced technology.

Nevertheless, as of 1840, the iron and steel industry increasingly used anthracite, especially in eastern Pennsylvania, which was rich in that material. This coal, which burns in short bursts of flame, required additional blasts of air.

In 1860, Pennsylvania accounted for half of the nation's iron production. Its rolling mills had already satisfied an enormous demand for iron rails, thanks especially to the Cambria Iron Works of Johnstown, where Kelly had attempted, but without success, to compete with the Bessemer process using a machine of his own design. The engineers John Fritz and Alexander L. Holley developed a metal-rolling process that made it possible to obtain low-cost rails of a uniform quality. By 1876, the Cambria Iron Company had become the foremost producer of steel rails in the United States. Near the end of the century, however, the narrow valleys of western Pennsylvania experienced competition from other sites of iron and steel production, especially along the banks of the Ohio River and the Great Lakes. Subsequently, Cambria was absorbed by Bethlehem Steel Company. The ten or so shops that have survived since the Johnstown site was shut down some twenty years ago evoke the transition from steel production in the artisanal era—when it was produced in small quantities and at great cost, to manufacture a limited number of tools—to the age of mass production. The octagonal brick forge, dating from 1864—used until a recent date, which explains its survival—housed the manufacturing equipment. The giant 1906 factory floor accommodated the machining of large metal parts.

From 1860 to 1919, Pennsylvania experienced staggering growth—jobs multiplied tenfold, production investments and value increased sixtyfold, and the number of industrial sites mushroomed—despite the fact that the state's share of national production dropped somewhat. That expansion coincided with the beginnings of the steel age, which occurred as the domestic demand for the construction of a railroad network intensified.

That conjunction is illustrated by the history of the Pennsylvania Railroad Company, which shows that on occasion the railroad companies attempted to seize control of the iron and steel industry in the interest of their own development. The company, created in 1846, had set the goal of connecting Philadelphia to Harrisburg, the state capital, and beyond it to the Great Lakes and the Gulf of Mexico, thus building an essential transportation and communication network. In 1849, the railroad reached Hollidaysburg and, in 1854, Pittsburgh, after the engineering achievement of Horseshoe Curve, west of Altoona, which made it possible to complete the crossing of the Allegheny mountain chain, the principal natural obstacle in the Appalachian system. The company, taking over a certain number of existing lines,

began to serve Chicago in 1855. The westward drive came about under the dynamic leadership of John Edgar Thomson.

A few years later, the Civil War required an extraordinary effort from the railroad network, and also gave steel rails the opportunity to demonstrate their superior resistance. The wrought-iron rail was doomed because it could not withstand heavy loads, and locomotives and their convoys were becoming increasingly weighty. Thus, in 1856 the Pennsylvania Railroad decided to undertake the production of steel by establishing the Pennsylvania Steel Company, for which it provided a third of the capital. In Steelton, south of Harrisburg, the new company set in operation the steel works and rolling mills that contributed to freeing the United States from its dependence on rails imported from Europe. The choice of location was judicious, since it allowed iron ore and coal of every kind, situated only a few dozen miles away, to arrive via the railroad company's convoys. Pennsylvania Steel in turn hired the services of the engineer Alexander Holley. This was the first very large American iron and steel complex, spread out over four miles along the Susquehanna River. By the 1870s, it was hard on the heels of Cambria in terms of its production.

In the 1870s, it was Pittsburgh and its industrial basin, which stretched the length of the Monongahela and Allegheny Rivers (whose junction formed the Ohio River), that experienced an extraordinary boom. Henry Clay Frick, founder of the Coal and Coke Company with the backing of Thomas Mellon, a Pittsburgh financier, took advantage of the deposits of bituminous coal in the region of Connellsville, on the western slope of the Appalachians, and gradually began to monopolize coke production. The voracious appetite of the Bessemer converters could no longer be satisfied with wood-fueled cast iron provided by traditional blast furnaces. That region, from 1860 until World War I, accounted for more than half the national production of coke, its capacity increasing from one thousand to forty thousand furnaces during that period. As for iron ore, it arrived from the Great Lakes via the newly constructed canals.

In considering the remarkable juncture of basic resources in the Pittsburgh area, the Monongahela River—somewhat like the Merrimack in a different time and a different technological

1

2

3

Above and right: *Johns Falls Valley factories and workers' houses in Baltimore, Maryland: 1) a single-family granite house (1840s) in the Stone Hill complex, near the Mount Vernon factory; 2) two-family wood cottages (late nineteenth century), near* *the Meadow Mill factory; 3) Druid Mill factory; 4) Meadow Mill and workers' row houses.*

Below: *The Enterprise Manufacturing Company in Augusta, Georgia.*

4

Above: *A model mill: the buildings of Sibley Manufacturing Company in Augusta, Georgia.*

Opposite: *The Eagle & Phenix Mills on the banks of the Chattahoochee River in Columbus, Georgia.*

Above: *The traditional brick Davol Mills (1867) in Fall River, Massachusetts.*

Opposite: *In the late nineteenth century, the use of granite quarry stone became common in the construction of the textile factories, which reached five to six stories in height. The symmetrical arrangement of the stairwells enhances the architectural quality of these massive structures in Fall River.*

Above and opposite: *After several decades of growth, the Amoskeag Manufacturing Company in Manchester, New Hampshire, had expanded to the dimensions of an industrial city arranged around a canal. The buildings follow the model of the original brick mills in New England, though obviously modernized.*

Opposite: *In Steelton, Pennsylvania, the workers at the Pennsylvania Steel Company gather around a Bessemer converter (about 1895). Visible on the upper level is the converter itself, a pear-shaped container that was tipped and filled with molten iron. Then it was returned to the upright position and cold air under high pressure was injected into it. The iron was thereby converted into steel, and a powerful combustion flame was given off. Notice the tank on the lower level, designed to collect the final product when the converter was tipped over.*

Left: *In about 1861–62, before the Bessemer converter was adopted, the Cambria Iron Works introduced the "Kelly steel converter," called the "pioneer converter in America," perfected in about 1850 and patented in 1855. The converter was installed in Johnstown in 1856, but the experiments were unsuccessful.*

Below: *The entrance to the shops of the Cambria Iron Works on the riverbank.*

Bottom: *The old Cambria shops still stretch along a narrow corridor next to the river.*

Above: *The skyscrapers of Pittsburgh, Pennsylvania, seen through Smithfield Bridge. Nothing remains of the old urban core, once liberally sprinkled with industrial complexes in the triangle formed by the confluence of the Monongahela and Allegheny Rivers.*

Right: *The Monongahela Valley south of Pittsburgh became a river transport corridor, serving convoys that directly loaded the coal brought from the nearby extraction sites.*

context—deserves special mention. In the 1810s, it had been the setting for the first experiments in steam navigation, by virtue of which New Orleans became the natural outlet of the Ohio basin. From the western slope of the central Appalachians, traders looked toward the Gulf of Mexico, not toward the ports of the North Atlantic coast; this has continued to be somewhat true even in our own time. Today, it is on the banks of the Monongahela in Brownsville that the only large business for the construction of boats for river navigation survives, the Hillman Barge & Construction Company. The river, its flow regulated by a whole system of dams and locks, became a key factor in the region's economic development, thanks to the inexpensive transport of coal extracted in abundance a short distance from its banks. Steam navigation was modernized in 1950 with the use of diesel-powered tugboats, which has made it possible for commerce there to maintain a regional, and even national role.

It was under these circumstances that the heads of the Cambria and the Pennsylvania companies, despite their efforts to control competition, could not prevent one of their rivals from moving to the foreground in 1880. Indeed, the history of steel in that region was henceforth dominated by Andrew Carnegie, a Scottish immigrant who had arrived in Pittsburgh in 1848. Carnegie, first employed at the Pennsylvania Railroad Company and founder of the Keystone Bridge Company in 1865, began manufacturing steel in 1873. In 1875, in Braddock, near Pittsburgh, he built the Edgar Thomson Factory, which combined a blast furnace, a steel works, and rolling mills for the production of rails. Once again, the complex was designed by the engineer Alexander Holley. Carnegie's strategy consisted of systematically buying out his competitors as soon as a new business was created. Thus, he became the owner of the Homestead factory in 1883, and later of the Duquesne factory, as he moved up the Monongahela, the axis of this new industrial empire. With his brother Thomas and with Frick, he formed two different companies, which he merged into Carnegie Steel in 1882. Through his association with Frick, he managed to control almost all the coke produced in the thousands of small furnaces in the region. In 1895, his crowning achievement was the con-

clusion of an agreement with John D. Rockefeller on the exploitation of iron ore in Michigan. Hence, a perfect integration of resources was set in place from Lake Superior to Pittsburgh, linked via a fleet of ore ships and port facilities on the Great Lakes, which were connected to the factories by railroad lines.

Nevertheless, a weary Carnegie sold his interests to J. P. Morgan in 1901. This gave birth to the U.S. Steel Company, which was the occasion for the creation, in 1906, of the last of the giant iron and steel complexes, located in Gary, Indiana, the large suburb south of Chicago. Today, the blast furnaces, now dormant, stand side by side with the most modern installations, which continue to produce steel. However, some day the same preservation issues will undoubtedly arise there that were raised in the Monongahela Valley, then in the Lehigh Valley, regarding the Bethlehem Steel Company.

Carnegie's thirty or so years of activity in the Pittsburgh region coincided with the appearance of a very capitalistic form of industry, which obeyed modern rules of management, employed even the most insignificant cost-cutting measures (developed in particular under the bookkeeping administration of Charles Schwab), and involved an intensive integration and automation of production and of the manipulation of raw materials. The dimensions of the blast furnaces grew, as did the power of the compressors and rolling mills. One of the blast furnaces of Carrie Furnaces illustrates the enormous leap forward realized during that period: the world record in daily cast-iron production was achieved in 1900, with eight hundred tons, compared to an average of fifty-five tons around 1872.

The might of the iron and steel industries spurred an incredible diversity of small industries around them. They produced all the metal equipment, tools, and structural components, from all sorts of hardware to bridges and locomotives. These developments anticipated the boom in electrical equipment produced by the Westinghouse factories and the beginning of the aluminum industry (Alcoa—Aluminum Company of America—was founded in New Kensington, on the Allegheny River, in 1907).

The boom was accompanied by a proliferation of industrial plants, of water and rail communication lines, and of working-class districts that swallowed up the rural environment of that region of Pennsylvania. At the time of the second industrial revolution, Pittsburgh, more than any other industrial center in the country, symbolized the progress of the American nation toward global industrial leadership. The painter Aaron Harry Gorson (1872–1933), who lived in Pittsburgh from 1903 to 1921, captured the city's somewhat terrifying image on canvases profoundly inspired by the aesthetic of Whistler, whom he had known during a stay in Paris. Gorson's interpretation of the strange beauty of landscapes composed of water, smoke, and steel reflects what this industrial world, which has now almost completely vanished, was like.

The Homestead Works in Homestead provided the steel necessary to build the Empire State Building in New York and the Sears Tower in Chicago and forged armor plating for generations of warships. The complex, which extended over five hundred acres, has been completely torn down. That quintessential working-class city preserves the memory of the July 1892 battle of Homestead, a bloody clash between the workers and the Pinkerton Guards recruited by Carnegie. The workers were armed with sticks, guns, burning oil, and dynamite, and had even obtained a cannon dating from the Civil War.

Somewhat farther to the south, the Duquesne Works were built between 1889 and 1894. Purchased by Carnegie in 1890 (and closed only in 1984), they were equipped with electric furnaces—and, more recently, with oxygen furnaces—for the production of steel. It was there that, in 1897, a revolutionary system for loading the blast furnaces mechanically—in other words, for automating the manipulation of raw materials—was inaugurated. The iron ore (or coke), unloaded via a traveling crane, was brought directly to a bucket elevator, which hoisted it to the upper opening of the blast furnace. In 1904, a battery of three hundred coke furnaces was built under the direction of Henry Clay Frick. They cooked the bituminous coal from the famous Pittsburgh seam, a vein of coal that extends into West Virginia. That form of coal replaced

anthracite and served to heat the open-hearth furnaces that were slower than the Bessemer converters, but which made it possible to process larger quantities, and which were better suited to manufacture certain products.

A public organization, the Regional Industrial Development Corporation, is currently attempting to promote an industrial park on that site. An 1899 rolling mill, equipped with forty-eight-inch rollers, was disassembled and stored, in the hope that it may be rebuilt in a steel heritage center, possibly housed at the former Carrie Furnaces. Not far from that site, straddling Turtle Creek, a small tributary of the Monongahela, the George Westinghouse Bridge stands perfectly intact, displaying five of the most majestic concrete arches in the United States from the 1930s. The bridge was named after the great builder whose first factories still dominate the city of Wilmerding, which underwent the phenomenal industrializing effects of coal, iron, and steel on the metropolitan industrial region of Pittsburgh. Farther to the east, Meadville and Jeannette also stand as witnesses to the era, supporting an active plate-glass and pressed-glass industry. That region has long been the leader of the glass industry in the United States, both in terms of its level of production and in its modern technology. Clearly, all the ingredients for a possible regional industrial heritage park are found in this area.

A section of the Monongahela Valley south of Duquesne was oriented around the factory of Clairton. There, U.S. Steel, Carnegie's successor, which had already increased its production capacity of coke by building hundreds of new furnaces in Gary in 1906 and around Connellsville in 1908, constructed 640 furnaces in 1916 to meet wartime demands. These now represent the most powerful battery in the United States. Their capacity has increased gradually, rising to nearly 1,600 furnaces. Clairton supplied the blast furnaces and steel works located downstream not only with coke, but also with recuperated hot gas, transported through an impressive network of air conduits. That was the decisive advantage of the new technique for distilling coal, compared to the traditional technique of cooking it in the old "beehive" ovens (a reference to their internal structure). This network

72

Top: *Carrie Furnaces, a solitary blast furnace in an enormous industrial wasteland in Homestead, Pennsylvania.*

Above: *Only a row of smokestacks remains of an old Homestead saw works, a well-maintained ruin located at the site of the ovens. At night, floodlights create the illusion of a temple colonnade.*

Right: *A mechanized system for loading the blast furnaces in operation at the Duquesne Works south of Homestead, another site of the U.S. Steel Company.*

Opposite: *The compressor room in one of the few large factories still in operation in Clairton, Pennsylvania, at the southern end of the Monongahela Valley's industrialized zone.*

Top: *The Clairton Works sits on the banks of the river that supplies coal to the enormous coking plant.*

Bottom right: *Shallow pits for coke ovens in the Pittsburgh region remain from the early days of the iron and steel industry in Pennsylvania.*

Opposite: *A row of steam-driven hammers at the factory of the Midvale Steel Company in Philadelphia, Pennsylvania.*

Above: *In the same factory, a shop for manufacturing molded-steel ship's anchors weighing four hundred pounds each, part of an order for 130 units by the U.S. Navy.*

remains connected to the Edgar Thomson unit, which benefited from the most advanced modern technology.

In about 1900, the Pittsburgh region concentrated forty percent of United States steel production along its thirty miles of riverways. Pennsylvania Steel had also continued its ascension, with its four large blast furnaces and its Bessemer converters. Between 1883 and 1893, it had also made the transition to open-hearth technology. In 1887, the company expanded to Baltimore, creating the Sparrows Point steel works and naval yards under the control of its subsidiary, the Maryland Steel Company. That plant, located at a strategic point on the Chesapeake Bay, made it possible to bring together iron ore imported from Cuba (following the 1882 discovery on that island of a deposit of high-grade ore) and the coal of central and western Pennsylvania. With the high demand brought about by World War I, Bethlehem Steel, needing to increase its production capacity, purchased Pennsylvania, Steelton, and Sparrows Point all at once, in 1916. In Philadelphia, the Midvale Steel Works specialized in supplying the large parts ordered by the U.S. Naval Yards.

During the same period, John Fritz was head of the Bethlehem Steel factory (near Allentown, Pennsylvania), where he improved the Bessemer process and then introduced heavy forging technology. Under Fritz the company became a cannon and armor-plate manufacturer for the first steel warships of the U.S. Navy, which served in the Spanish-American War of 1898. He has therefore been considered one of the creators of the so-called military-industrial complex.

It was through that manufacturing operation that ties were established between the French Schneider firm of Le Creusot and Bethlehem Steel. In fact, the U.S. government recognized the supremacy of the technology of homogeneous steel that Le Creusot had been working on since 1875 and placed orders for it with Bethlehem Steel, which collaborated with Schneider to organize its manufacture. It built a 130-ton power hammer, based on the Le Creusot model, to forge armor. The perfection of nickel-plated steel marked yet another phase of this development. At the tests conducted at the shooting range in Annapolis, Mary-

land, site of the U.S. Naval Academy, an American commission rated Schneider as the best, ahead of Cammel, from Sheffield, after a French armor plate ten-and-a-half inches thick resisted shots without perforating or splitting, and even shattered three projectiles.

The Bethlehem factory, built in 1887 on the banks of the Lehigh River, devoted itself to filling manufacturing orders for the military. Bethlehem Steel, along with its naval yards, represented the government's principal partner in the war effort during the two world wars. Today, the factory is almost completely shut down. Bethlehem Steel still has its offices there, and production continues in the Steelton factory, in the naval yards of Baltimore, and in Hunt's Point, Indiana. But the total number of workers has fallen from three hundred thousand in about 1945 to fifteen thousand. Nevertheless, the Bethlehem plants still stand along five miles of the Lehigh. In the twentieth century, the factory made a specialty of manufacturing large steel girders for the construction of skyscrapers and long-span bridges (the Golden Gate Bridge in San Francisco, for example). The heads of the company like to say that, if the Bethlehem steel supporting New York were removed from it, two-thirds of the city would collapse.

Therefore, one should not underestimate the value of the iron and steel industry in the United States as fundamental historical evidence of the formation of methods of production and socioeconomic structures since the 1860s. That branch of industry has been evolving constantly, in both economic and technological terms, as a result of a dynamic process of interaction between consumers and producers, and as a function of the successive or simultaneous need for different products. Rails, metal frames for bridges or skyscrapers, armor plating, steel for the automobile industry, and so on—all were needed.

The truly colossal size of most of the installations leaves open the question of how to maintain and adapt that iron and steel heritage, which has considerable historical and symbolic significance. Up to now the only experiment in heritage preservation in this industrial sector has occurred in the South, with the Sloss Furnaces of Birmingham, Alabama. These furnaces are contemporaneous with the great iron and steel plants in the northern states but are more modest in size (they occupy only seventeen acres). They owe their name to their owner and founder, James Sloss, an astute Irish businessman. Built and put into operation between 1881 and 1884, they benefited from the introduction in the United States of a British technology for recuperating gas. They were modernized between 1927 and 1931 and shut down in 1971. This site, representative of the mass production of cast iron used in the manufacture of pipes, made Birmingham the principal American supplier of that product in the mid-twentieth century. Another characteristic of the site is that it prospered due to the efforts of a plentiful unskilled black labor force. Until the early twentieth century, these black workers performed very hard and dangerous work, which consisted of loading the blast furnaces from a platform located at the top.

NAVAL YARDS AND ARSENALS

Naval yards and arsenals have been an important aspect of the industrial heritage of the United States since the nation's birth. Their preservation is considered to be a priority by those in the government and the general population who recognize their great national significance.

The Charleston Navy Yard, located on the banks of the Charles River, near the port of Boston, is a jewel of our military, industrial, and technological heritage. It operated from 1800 to 1974 and, during all that time, was responsible for the construction, repair, and rehabilitation of thousands of ships. At its largest, it occupied one hundred and thirty acres with eighty-six buildings, and was served by some five miles of railroad lines and by a forest of cranes near the piers and dry docks. During World War II, Charleston employed as many as fifty thousand workers and launched a ship a month. Its shutdown in 1974 was consistent with its obsolescence, when compared to the modern techniques of naval construction, but left five thousand unemployed. The buildings, most of which have been preserved, offer a striking variety of architectural features, determined by their time of

construction and their technical use. The structures are organized around a regular grid of streets—carefully laid out and landscaped—which have become city roads. Among the most famous of these buildings is the Ropewalk, with a floor space fifteen hundred feet long (corresponding to the length of the longest ropes manufactured), built in 1834–37 by Alexander Parris; it owes a debt to its European ancestors in Rochefort and Venice. The 1903 Chain and Forge Shop, beginning in 1928, produced anchor chains that were authorized by the U.S. Navy and considered the most resistant in the world: the components of each link were forged together with a hammer specially invented for that purpose.

The Watervliet Arsenal, in Albany County, New York, dates from 1813, around the time of the second war of independence. Its location was selected because of the excellent service via canals—then via railroad—that it enjoyed in the early days of its expansion. Later, its operations were spurred by the Mexican War in the 1840s and the Civil War. In 1889, it became a government facility that manufactured large-caliber artillery, particularly cannons for coastal defense installed along the Panama Canal and in Manila Bay, and it grew again during the two world wars.

In every period, the vast factory floors required by this type of industry, and by the protective measures required for it to operate, led to the use of the most advanced techniques. Such was the case, for example, of an armory built in 1859 under the administration of Major Alfred Mordecai, a military engineer and graduate of West Point, with the cooperation of the civil engineer Daniel Badger.

World War I, given the unprecedented scope of the orders for armaments and the related developments in architecture for industrial use, produced structures of astounding scale. In Bridgeport, Connecticut—one of the cities most affected by de-industrialization along the northeastern coast of the United States—two unique buildings attest to this fact. One is the factory built by Remington, within an eight-month period in 1915, to satisfy a Russian order for 1 million guns and $100 million of munitions, at a time when other establishments were having difficulty filling the British orders. Even today it extends over a

Top: *The first office building of the Bethlehem Iron Company in Bethlehem, Pennsylvania, about 1863 (picture by Johnson Yerkes). Although it remained fairly modest in size, the company, under John Fritz's leadership, was one of the pioneers in the manufacture of Bessemer steel in the 1870s. In 1899, Charles Schwab purchased the company and transformed it into what was at one time the second-largest steel works in the United States. Beginning in 1908, the firm became a major supplier of steel for skyscrapers and other large construction projects. During the two World Wars, it also supplied armor plate and large-caliber cannons for the Navy. In 1985, plans were made to end steel production by 1995.*

Above: *A partial view of the Bethlehem factories, showing the blast furnace towers as they appeared in 1883.*

Opposite: *An aerial view of the Bethlehem steel works on the banks of the Lehigh River in the 1930s. The first factory was built there in 1857 to produce rails; production began in 1863. Bessemer steel was produced there beginning in the 1870s.*

LEHIGH VALLEY FREIGHT STATION

Above: *The interior of the cannon-drilling shop at the Bethlehem factories. As in the case of the ship's anchor shop in Midvale (see page 77), this is a superb example of a large shop with an entirely metal frame.*

Right: *Loading sheet metal onto rail cars at the Bethlehem factories.*

Opposite: *A hydraulic press for compressing steel to make it more homogeneous, suitable for the manufacture of armor plating or large pieces of artillery.*

Top: *Forging an article with a power hammer at the Bethlehem factories in the early twentieth century. Compared to the hydraulic press, which was more automated, the earlier technology of the steam-powered hammer required a whole team to operate it.*

Bottom: *The mid-sized power hammer shop at the Le Creusot factories in France. Note the similarity between the tools used at the turn of the twentieth century on both sides of the Atlantic.*

Opposite: *A publicity image of the traditional power hammer at the Bethlehem plant. This nonworking model was created for the World's Columbian Exposition in Chicago in 1893.*

The compressor room at the Bethlehem factories. The monumental scale of industry is demonstrated not only in the building's vast dimensions but also in the multiple rows of equipment.

Left: *Releasing the flow of molten metal from the blast furnace at the Bethlehem factories.*

Below: *The press shop at the Bethlehem factories where an article being forged is cut out.*

Opposite, top left: *The row of smokestacks in the old steel works, photographed from the top of a furnace in Bethlehem, Pennsylvania.*

Opposite, top right: *An electric oven and ingot molds.*

Opposite, bottom: *The coke ovens at night, three days before they were shut down. A 1997 agreement between Bethlehem and the Smithsonian Institution stipulated that a museum and a commercial complex be created on part of the factory site.*

Left: *The ramp and the loading buckets of blast furnace No. 2 at Sloss Furnaces, installed in Birmingham, Alabama, in 1927.*

Opposite: *A double row of boiler chimneys, framing a horizontal cylinder for scrubbing the gases and, in the background, blast furnace No. 1 at the Sloss Furnaces.*

Above: *An early-nineteenth-century shop at the Boston shipyards, with the dry dock in the foreground.*

Right: *Building No. 110, the shop for the coastal defense artillery, at the Watervliet arsenal in Albany County, New York. The exterior of the building is made of brick, in the tradition of the large metallurgical shops of the nineteenth century. Although the arsenal was built during the War of 1812, it experienced its real growth with the Mexican War and the Civil War (1848–65). In 1889, it became the federal government's cannon factory.*

Opposite: *Building No. 110 at Watervliet in about 1900, (see previous double page), with its powerful steel frame supporting traveling cranes weighing 240 to 265 tons. Watervliet became famous for its specialization in very large caliber cannons for coastal defense. Before World War I (1914–18), they were sold especially for the defense of the Panama Canal and Manila Bay.*

Above: *A destroyer is dry-docked for the purpose of modernization in the U.S. Navy shipyards at League Island in Philadelphia, Pennsylvania.*

Top: *The first Ford factory (1904–10), birthplace of the Model T, on Piquette Avenue in Detroit, Michigan. The plant was built in the traditional style of nineteenth-century New England: a long and narrow three-story building.*

Bottom: *One of the shops of the Ford factory in Highland Park (Detroit) in 1909. It was Albert Kahn's first commission from Henry Ford. This six-story building inaugurated the "rational" factory, which saved on labor through the use of a large number of machines arranged in sequential order and revolutionized the handling of materials and parts through trucks, inclines, conveyors, and electric cranes.*

Opposite: *A 385-ton crane in the Philadelphia shipyards.*

The Ford plant in Highland Park (1914): in the center, the thermal plant; on either side, office buildings. The rational factory plan was the culmination of a tradition that can be traced to Oliver Evans. It is also indebted to the instruction given at the Massachusetts Institute of Technology in the 1880s regarding the interior and exterior design of factories, and to scientific management theory as Frederick Taylor defined it.

space twenty-five hundred feet long; it has thirteen five-story modules, arranged in an H-shape, all isolated from one another (to keep the damage from spreading in the event of an explosion), with brick and concrete walls sixteen inches thick, narrow communicating doors cut into the walls, and wood floors ten inches thick. The main facade, along the width of the building, is a superb example of a so-called daylight factory, an architectural design that exposes the production floors to natural light as much as possible, in the interest of the work and of the workers themselves.

The Philadelphia Navy Yard, the only plant of this type still operating on the East Coast, began to expand on the site beginning in 1871, eventually occupying nearly eight hundred acres. Its growth occurred in tandem with the Spanish-American War and the two world wars. During World War II, this naval yard employed forty-seven thousand workers. The dimensions of the modern warships required a no less impressive scale in the most recent buildings, where the influence of functional architecture, previously developed to meet the needs of the automobile and aeronautics industries, can be seen.

THE TWENTIETH-CENTURY FACTORY: MASS CONSUMPTION AND THE RATIONALIZATION OF WORK

In the late nineteenth century, the industrial geography of the United States underwent a decisive shift linked to the emergence of the automobile and aeronautics industries. Already, from Pittsburgh to Buffalo to Chicago, and including Cleveland, Akron, and Toledo, a chain of regional metropolises formed that counterbalanced the industrial centers of the original thirteen colonies. In that chain, the primary link for the next half-century was Detroit, where the automobile industry originated. That industry gave rise to a true industrial revolution, which also translated into a new organization of work (Chicago had already provided a model in its meat-processing plants) and a new industrial architecture.

Detroit's glory years were 1910 to 1930. In 1929, 5.3 million automobiles were produced, and half the city's labor force worked in the industry. Spurred by a tremendous immigration movement, the population had swelled from under 300,000 in 1900 to more than 1.5 million in 1929. At that time, Detroit became the foremost industrial center in the United States.

Contrary to a commonly held notion, it was not Henry Ford who created the automobile industry, but rather Ransom Olds. Olds, after selling his first automobile in New York in 1893, moved to Detroit in 1899. He was the inventor of the first inexpensive, mass-produced car. At the time, automobile workers did no more than assemble the components provided by subcontractors such as Dodge, Timken, and Uniroyal. But it was Ford who adopted the idea of focusing primarily on one mass-produced product with his Model T (a code name assigned by the design department), launched in 1908 and nicknamed the "Tin Lizzie." Nearly 15 million cars were produced in the twenty years of the Model T's existence (1908–27); following World War I, more than one new car in two produced in the United States was a Ford Model T. In addition, Ford decided to begin manufacturing all the auto parts on a single site.

Henry Ford's well-known quip, "Any customer can have a car painted any color that he wants so long as it is black," alludes to his extraordinary innovations. Before Ford revolutionized the industry, cars were luxury items, manufactured to order, according to the customer's taste, and produced by hundreds of small artisan brands. Ford inaugurated the single-model car, which was both technologically advanced and inexpensive to buy, thanks to mass production and the economy of scale.

This new type of industry gave birth to a new architecture, which arose from the entirely original solutions to Ford's unprecedented demands by the architect and engineer Albert Kahn. A thirty-year intellectual exchange closely united these two self-made men, both born in 1860, even though Ford was an anti-Semite and Kahn, a humble Jewish immigrant.

The Ford Model T was first produced in Highland Park, then a suburb of Detroit. Built in 1909, the concrete factory building was several stories high, and the assembly of the car's components took place from top to bottom, with the car rolling out on the ground floor, ready to be tested. Fifteen years later, the engineer Matté Trucco built the Fiat factory in Lingotto, Turin, a giant reinforced-concrete building that paid homage to the Highland Park model. Conversely, at the Fiat plant, the fully assembled car rolled out onto the factory roof, which had been designed as a test track. Once tested, the automobile was sent down to the ground via a monumental spiral ramp.

The Ford project was not the first order Albert Kahn had received from the automobile industry. In 1903, he had worked for Henry B. Joy, president of Packard. The construction of shop no. 10 in 1905 had given him the opportunity to use concrete, an inexpensive material that was very solid and noncombustible, guaranteeing great stability as well as rapid construction—a necessary consideration given the growth of the market. In addition, the use of concrete made it possible to adapt a factory's layout to the needs of automobile construction by freeing up the floor space with fewer load-bearing supports. In Packard shop no. 10, the interior columns were spaced thirty feet apart, an unusually large span at the time. A more flexible space made it possible to experiment with new ways to organize the production process and demonstrated that henceforth the architect would be more concerned with the interior function of the space than with a quest for an architectural style for the facades. The walls were characterized by enormous windows, occupying the large openings that were determined by the grid of the concrete frame. Multipaned metal-framed windows were the dominant feature of the building's exterior.

"Architecture is 90 percent business and 10 percent art," Albert Kahn was in the habit of saying. As for Ford, he was not looking for an architectural marvel to celebrate the entrepreneur in the form of a new industrial aesthetic, but rather a design able to provide practical solutions to the specific needs of mass production. Thus, it is easy to understand the success of the collaboration between Ford and Kahn.

The first Ford assembly line was installed on Piquette Avenue, in a building poorly suited to the assembly of the future

Model T. Ford ordered a four-story shop, nearly a thousand feet long and only eighty feet wide. The change in scale was radical, compared to Packard shop no. 10. The facade had brick stairwells at regular intervals, which also housed elevators and restrooms for the workers. The load-bearing concrete structure rested on framing members only twenty feet wide, with no intermediate supporting wall. It was in this very open space that the assembly line was perfected and finally became operational in 1913: chassis on the ground floor, auto bodies on the second floor, with the preliminary operations taking place on the third and fourth floors. Enormous windows occupied almost all the openings in the concrete frame, thus responding to Henry Ford's requirements regarding the optimal conditions for lighting and ventilation. His concern for cleanliness was no less keen: seven hundred employees were responsible for cleaning the shops, washing the windows, and repainting. This was the expression of his conviction that the quality of the work environment could positively affect the workers' attitudes toward their tasks.

During a second phase of development in the mid-1910s, Ford abandoned the multistory factory concept in favor of a single-level organization of work. Even though Albert Kahn used the Highland Park model again in 1921 for the Fisher Body Company factory in Cleveland, he followed Ford's programmatic demands in their next collaboration. Thus, on two occasions, he played an essential role in the evolution of an important industrial building type: first, in the development of the multistoried concrete-frame structure, and second, in the construction of buildings on a single level, primarily using a steel framework.

In the first stage, the Highland Park plant was integrated into a set of buildings, each of which specialized in a different operation. That meant abandoning the principle of performing all the phases under one roof, or rather, it meant making each building a component in a sort of segmented assembly line. In 1906 Kahn had already experimented with the single-level factory in the construction of the buildings of the Pierce plant in Buffalo, in collaboration with Lockwood, Greene & Martin of Boston, to whom he introduced the entirely new technique of building con-

Above: *The Fisher Body factory in Detroit, Michigan.*

Left: *One of the buildings of the Packard factory in Detroit (1907).*

Opposite, top: *The iron and steel section of Ford's River Rouge plant south of Detroit.*

Opposite, bottom: *The River Rouge plant, developed between 1917 and 1938, was Albert Kahn's second commission from Henry Ford. The canal and port are at the very center of the plant. Exemplifying the last phase in the evolution of the rational factory, the horizontal plant was planned on a single level and spread out among a great number of buildings on a huge site.*

The Curtiss-Wright aircraft factory in Buffalo (1945). A factory of vast open spaces, it was converted after World War II to manufacture electric engines for civilian use.

Right: *The assembly hangar of the Glenn Martin aircraft factory in Baltimore, Maryland (1937).*

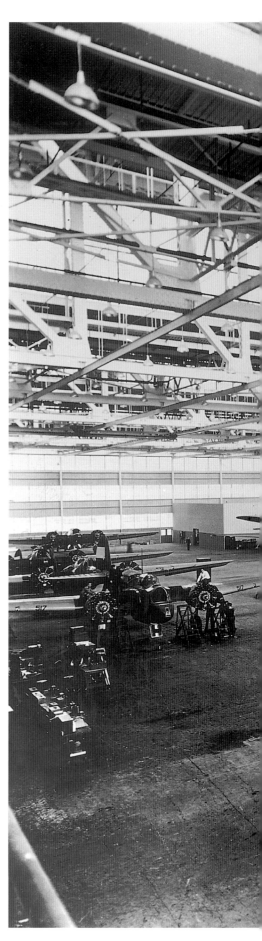

12022

crete factories. These were seven low buildings, each corresponding to one phase of manufacturing. Thus, Ford and Kahn simply perfected a model.

The new site chosen by Ford was River Rouge, a few miles from Detroit. The essential prerequisite for the site was the construction of a canal linking the site to the Detroit River, and hence to the Great Lakes, which was able to accommodate freighters. Building construction proper began in 1917 (continuing until 1939), in conjunction with a submarine order for the U.S. Navy; thus was born Eagle Plant, a building more than sixteen hundred feet long. The area covered by the most varied shops, which assured the business's self-sufficiency, rose from two thousand acres at the outset—acreage acquired at low cost—to nearly thirteen square miles. The internal port and a network of ninety miles of railways guaranteed the quickest circulation of materials and products, in order to shorten the manufacturing time as much as possible. The floor space was considerably expanded compared to the Highland Park factory, thanks to the use of steel components for the roofs and interior columns, which were now very thick and spaced at a great distance from one another. The parts entered at one end of the building and the car came out finished on the other, having traveled along a single moving assembly line, which was supplied laterally along the way with all the necessary components.

Albert Kahn, a revolutionary in industrial-use architecture, built about two thousand factories between 1900 and 1940, but without achieving recognition from his peers, who had little respect for utilitarian buildings that did not fit within the canon of public, civic, and residential architecture. However, he succeeded in focusing the attention of corporate customers on his Detroit firm, which still operates under the name Albert Kahn Associates. Kahn worked in the service of a great number of automobile manufacturers, and later of manufacturers in the aeronautics industry. Thus, he worked for Glenn Martin in Middle River, north of Baltimore, in 1929, 1937, 1939, and 1941, and in Omaha, Nebraska, in 1941. In 1937, Glenn Martin, convinced that the wingspan of airplanes would soon reach three hundred feet,

commissioned from Kahn an unobstructed space measuring three hundred by one hundred and fifty feet, with one end entirely open for the finished airplane to exit through. Albert Kahn borrowed bridge technology to design steel trusses of a size previously unequaled.

Similar requirements of the techniques of industrial architecture had already been taken into account in Akron, Ohio, in 1929, with the construction of Goodyear Airdock, the largest dirigible shop and hangar in the world. That parabolic steel structure, designed to house the erection of the large airships ordered by the U.S. Navy from the Goodyear-Zeppelin Corporation, still inspires awe by virtue of its dimensions (twelve hundred feet long, three hundred and thirty feet wide, two hundred and ten feet high) and its vast, open floor space. The largest semis look like toys at its yawning entrance.

In 1939, Glenn Martin called for a second unit contiguous to the first, and Albert Kahn completed it between February 5 and April 23. Wartime production further increased the pressure on his firm, which was responsible for the Willow Run factory in Ypsilanti, Michigan, which in 1943 was the largest war factory in the world (forty-two thousand workers). Designed for the construction of Ford's B-24 bomber, the structure was more than half a mile long and thirteen hundred feet across at its widest. In addition, many orders were filled in Chicago, Illinois; Louisville, Kentucky; New Orleans, Louisiana; and other sites. Within the context of a military program that required minimal delays, the standardization of architectural solutions became a key advantage.

Another, no less fundamental revolution initiated by Kahn lay in the essential change in the architect's relation to his projects and to his client. Traditionally, the nineteenth-century architect superimposed decorated facades and eclectic forms on buildings designed to house industrial work. Later, architects of a more modern spirit, who were passionate about technology and engineering, gave the factory an avant-garde structure, but were unable to refrain from applying references to styles borrowed from other periods—hence, Peter Behrens evoked a Greek temple in the design of the AEG turbine factory in Berlin. In both cases, the architect was faithful to a system of artistic and aesthetic sources, and to the intention of making the industrial building a pretext for the discovery of new forms containing new symbols.

Conversely, Albert Kahn's phenomenal commercial success can be explained by the relation he was able to establish with many Detroit businessmen, in a city where he had learned his trade, and with the engineers trained at the University of Michigan. His practical approach was to submit completely to the technical and economic requirements of the entrepreneurs and to the dictates of the new organization of work. Kahn's capacity to satisfy the demand of industries that required large amounts of space, and which had an almost frenetic growth rate, proved to be astounding. His success can be attributed to his firm's organizational principle, in which work was entirely rationalized, from the design and supply of materials to the smallest detail of plumbing. Hence, Kahn came to surpass all other architectural engineering firms of the time.

One of Albert Kahn's greatest contributions rests, finally, in the ties that he established between the modernization of industrial production equipment and its architectural housing on the one hand, and the design of the city itself on the other. Following World War I, Kahn was the prime contractor of the new center city in Detroit. This district was designed to accommodate all the corporate headquarters for the new automobile industry, in buildings dedicated to displaying the glory of postwar economic growth. Kahn, who continued to take commissions from a very diverse clientele outside the narrow field of industry, was an excellent architect with eclectic tastes who used all the resources he had at his disposal.

PART 2

Major Themes in the Industrial Heritage of the United States

CHAPTER 3

Civil Engineering Takes Command

The settlement of the United States, spurred by successive waves of immigration and the professed initiative of westward expansion, was destined to take control of the continent. That conquest mobilized much of the expertise and theoretical research of the country's civil engineers, who were faced with the particular challenge of crossing waterways and large mountain ranges.

In that mobilization, craftsmen provided their knowledge of tools, materials, and the terrain. Engineers, military and civil, developed more formalized, mathematical models. The combination of these various talents made it possible to develop a whole range of solutions for surmounting the natural obstacles, all of them remarkable for their inventiveness, their efficiency, and their moderate cost. Hence, a true technological culture was forged in the United States, borrowing from abroad yet marked by great ingenuity and originality.

CANALS

As historical monuments, canals have made an impact on the American sensibility since the nineteenth century, a sensibility expressed by painters, poets, and photographers. Canals continue to fascinate people: the success of books illustrating their history attests to this phenomenon. The Easton Museum in Pennsylvania, at the confluence of the Delaware and Lehigh Rivers, is the site of an active canal-history society.

Canal-building experienced a very brief but intense golden age prior to 1850. From 1790 to 1860, 2 million dollars were spent to build thirty-two hundred miles of canals. Their infrastructures are still somewhat intact, sometimes in their entirety, but more often in segments. In their profile and their equipment, these canals are reminiscent of the European canals built beginning in the late eighteenth century.

Canals brought about a transformation of the American

A detail of the support structure on the east side of the George Washington Bridge in New York.

landscape by determining the location of activities and settlements in terms of land-use patterns known as *metropolitan corridors.* Beginning in the first half of the nineteenth century, canals were a driving force of economic life, mobilizing, on a large scale, private and public capital, battalions of semi-skilled and poorly paid migrant labor (freed blacks, and later Irish immigrants), and construction materials. They promoted the growth of the young American economy by helping it carve out a place on world markets, which was accomplished by reducing transportation costs between the regions of production and the industrial centers or maritime ports devoted to exportation.

Only the northeastern United States experienced the development of a relatively dense network of canals; the later phases of settlement were instead supported by the construction of the railroad network. Of these navigable waterways, some established the link between the Atlantic and the Great Lakes region, while others performed a more localized economic role.

The preeminent American canal was certainly the Erie, built over three hundred fifty miles between 1817 and 1825, partly opened in 1823, later widened from 1836 to 1863, and again between 1905 and 1917. It was the first success, setting off a speculative craze that could be called *canalmania,* and which made it possible to accelerate the opening of several regions of the country to commerce and industry. The construction of the Erie Canal was also the opportunity for an important transfer of technology between the Old and New Worlds in the field of civil engineering; thus, during a trip to England, the engineer Canvass White (the inventor of hydraulic cement and planner of the water distribution center in Cohoes) became well acquainted with the latest technology for installing canals.

The Erie Canal opened up the nation's interior by connecting Lake Erie and the Hudson River near Albany. The navigable Hudson ended in New York, and it was due to the canal that this city became the largest in the East and the major gateway to long-distance maritime trade. A commercial area and maintenance shops developed around the starting point of the canal's navigable zone, traces of which are preserved in the historic warehouse district of Troy. In Waterford, workshops, warehouses, and a dry dock supplied the canal with the hardware and construction materials needed to build the gates of fifty-seven locks, and to repair the dredges, tugboats, barges, and buoys.

At its other end, at Lake Erie, the great industrial center of Buffalo developed, a city destined to become the major distribution site for the grain and other agricultural products coming from the American plains. The canal followed the valley of the Mohawk River, a tributary of the Hudson that never benefited from the proximity of the Finger Lakes, natural reservoirs that were indispensable for feeding the canal.

The Ohio & Erie Canal bore many similarities to the Erie. Built between 1825 and 1832, it connected Portsmouth, on the Ohio River, to Cleveland, on Lake Erie, passing through Akron as of 1827. It played the role of catalyst in the economic development of the eastern part of Ohio and opened the way for the settlement of the regions it passed through. First used primarily for the transport of agricultural products, it took on much greater scope during the second half of the nineteenth century, connecting the Great Lakes to the iron, steel, and coal industries of Pittsburgh by conveying iron ore from Lake Superior. Cleveland's commercial and industrial center was located on a floodplain at the mouth of the Cuyahoga River known as "The Flats," which was gradually invaded by docks, warehouses, railroad facilities, factories of all kinds, and later by the iron and steel industry.

In Akron, locks ten to eighteen of the Ohio & Erie Canal were the major site of the city's industrialization in the nineteenth and twentieth centuries, as demonstrated by the Cascade Mills (1876), which later become the property of Quaker Oats (1910–40). At that site, thirty-six concrete grain elevators, each one hundred twenty feet high and some twenty feet in diameter, have been converted into a Hilton Hotel with two hundred circular rooms and a recreation center. A series of seven locks nearby has become Cascade Locks Park.

Another rival of the Erie Canal was the Chesapeake & Ohio Canal. The company of the same name, founded in 1825, planned to link Washington, D.C. (more accurately, Georgetown) to Pittsburgh, which was called the "gateway to the West" because of its position at the head of the Ohio Valley. The project planned to exploit the only easy crossing point of the Appalachians southwest of the Hudson-Mohawk Valley, at Cumberland, Maryland, at the foot of the chain's eastern peaks.

But the canal, begun in 1828 and completed in 1850, never got past Cumberland. That failure occurred, significantly, due to the contemporaneous construction of the National Road, ordered by Congress in 1806 and opened between Cumberland and Wheeling in 1818, and that of the Baltimore & Ohio Railroad, beginning in the 1830s.

The decision of the U.S. Congress to move forward with road building can be explained by the desire to promote westward expansion. At the time, the easiest passage across the Appalachians had been identified as being at the western end of Maryland, and the members of Congress had begun to remedy the deplorable state of the road network, which was merely a collection of muddy paths that deteriorated every season. By 1800, most of the states had not yet begun the construction of paved roads. Established between 1811 and 1818, the National Road, still called "Uncle Sam's Road" and now Route 40, was the first interstate in the history of the United States. Despite having to transfer cargo at two points, in Wheeling and Brownsville (where the road intersected the Monongahela River), trade along the road almost immediately became so heavy that it had to be rebuilt more solidly in 1829.

The first large national public works project, the National Road played a pioneering role in the internal expansion of the country, bringing about a corridor of settlement running through Ohio, Indiana, Illinois, and on to Mississippi. In the end, however, it lost its federal support and suffered a great deal from competition with the railroads. It is, nevertheless, a true cultural landscape today, distinguished by its layout, its architecture, and its feats of engineering. As for the B&O Railroad, it made the National Road obsolete as a transportation axis and contributed toward the termination of the canal, which had the disadvantage of freezing up in the winter.

The canal did serve a function, however, becoming an excellent means for removing coal from the mines in western Maryland via the upper Potomac Valley. That traffic in coal reached its peak in 1875, before declining rapidly. It fed all the ports on the northeastern coast of the United States, and later the ports of Panama and even San Francisco, where the cargo was exported to sites as distant as the Far East.

The construction of the canal began in Georgetown; between 1831 and 1845, it was extended about seven miles to the port of Alexandria, where traders feared having their traditional role as importers of all sorts of supplies, destined for the outlying regions, supplanted by Georgetown. (Alexandria had been a base of operations and of resupply during the Seven Years' War, especially during Braddock's offensive against the French position of Fort Duquesne, near Pittsburgh.) But the construction of this extension was laborious: it had to cross the Potomac to Williamsport, near Washington, D.C., on a canal bridge one thousand feet long; then, four locks had to be built to bring the canal back up to the level of the docks and warehouses in the seaport. This notorious bridge was damaged as a result of its closure during the Civil War, when it was covered over and used as a road bridge for the passage of troops. The cracks that had formed in the structure led to it being definitively closed.

The history of the Chesapeake & Ohio Canal presents an opportunity to consider what can happen when canals become obsolete. They have generally been subjected to every sort of indignity: the stone of the locks and basins has been reused, industrial waste or garbage has been dumped into them, or the layout of the beds has been coopted by the railways. But, with the help of the economic expansion of the 1980s, an exemplary cooperation between the public and private sectors, between archaeologists and urban planners, has made it possible to excavate and restore one lock and one tidal basin in Alexandria. Large numbers of beams and boards that had remained intact were able to be exhumed. An urban canal park was integrated into the city plan, and the Alexandria Waterfront Museum has made the canal accessible to the public.

The benefits that the Erie Canal offered the state and city of New York also produced worries among Pennsylvania's members of Congress, who, in 1824, began to plan a canal that would link Philadelphia to Pittsburgh; work began in 1826. The Susquehannah River, which flows into Chesapeake Bay, appeared to be a natural line of communication, but in reality its valley was only a corridor heading in a southerly direction, whereas the crossing of the Appalachians required an east–west passage. In an effort to accomplish that crossing, builders took advantage of the valley of the Juniata River, a tributary on the east side of the Susquehannah, with the confluence located upstream of Harrisburg. But, beyond that, the extension of the canal ran up against the chain of the Allegheny Mountains, which could only be crossed with the help of a series of inclined planes, later made obsolete by the railroad. Further on, navigation toward the Allegheny River and Pittsburgh could resume. Thus, the Pennsylvania Canal was no greater a success than the Chesapeake & Ohio. It was the promoters of the Pennsylvania Railroad Company, formed in 1846, who, between 1847 and 1854, finally established a truly unified connection, the first stage of what one of its presidents considered "a road established by nature to put New York and New Orleans in communication." So ended the dream of an entirely navigable link between the East Coast and the Mississippi basin, which had promised incomparable commercial prosperity, and which each of the large port cities on the Atlantic shore had hoped to exploit.

In about 1830, more than twelve hundred miles of canals were under construction in eastern Pennsylvania. The goal in every case was to guarantee an outlet for the anthracite mines in the industrial centers of New Jersey, New York, and Philadelphia. Anthracite was used for heating homes, manufacturing steam, and smelting iron—all in all, it represented an enormous market. Along the way, this coal would make Pennsylvania the heart of the iron industry in the United States. A network of canals was formed around the Lehigh Canal, which opened to navigation in 1818 and was closed in 1940, and the canal from the Delaware to the Hudson, built between 1827 and 1832 and closed in 1931. These

Opposite, top: *A bridge across the Schoharie River on the Erie Canal, near Auriesville, New York. Among the remarkable features of this canal, now unfortunately reduced to a number of segments more or less in ruins, were the canal bridges. Here, the freestone structure was composed of a series of short-span arches.*

Opposite, bottom: *The Delaware Aqueduct in Pennsylvania illustrates a different bridge technology, used for the Delaware and Hudson Canal: the suspension bridge made it possible to have wide openings between support piers, and thus did not obstruct navigation.*

Top left: *Crossing the Allegheny Mountains with the help of an incline, which made it possible to winch up boats onto glides between two sections of the canal.*

Above left: *A small railroad museum on a siding of the Jim Thorpe Station in Pennsylvania.*

Above right: *The entrance to the Blue Ridge Tunnel in Afton, Virginia. It was built by the French engineer Claudius Crozet, a member of the faculty at West Point from 1816 to 1823, then a civil engineer of canal and railroad projects in Virginia and Louisiana, and one of the founders of the Virginia Military Institute. Designed to traverse the principal chain of the Appalachians, this tunnel was the longest in the United States when built, and the first to have been drilled without the use of vertical shafts.*

*The principal facade of the former Pennsylvania Station in Manhattan, designed
in the majestic style of many public buildings at the turn of the twentieth century.*

Opposite: *The main hall of Pennsylvania Station.*

Above: *The Mount Clare locomotive roundhouse in Baltimore, Maryland, before its restoration. From the beginning, the introduction of a railroad line to link the Eastern seaboard to the interior of the United States received the ardent support of distinguished individuals and capitalists in Baltimore. For a long time the shops at the Mount Clare site, of which the roundhouse is a part, were the largest in the world, but they were later surpassed by those in Martinsburg, West Virginia.*

Right: *Pennsylvania Station in Baltimore, as it appears today.*

Opposite: *The former Pennsylvania Station in Philadelphia. There were once as many as eighty-five thousand railroad stations in the United States. About twelve thousand remained in the early 1990s.*

Left: *The locomotive round-house in Martinsburg, West Virginia. Unfortunately, only one of the two round-houses survives. They made a significant contribution to the efforts of the pioneering B&O Railroad company in its crossing of the Appalachian Mountains.*

Below: *The metal structure of the dome of the Martinsburg roundhouse.*

Left: *The passenger station of the Georgia Railroad in Savannah. This building dates from 1876, and its beautiful facade is now the entrance to the visitors' center at the rehabilitated site.*

Right: *The covered train platform, dating from 1861, and its wood-frame roof.*

Below: *The exterior of the same building.*

The large warehouse of the B&O Railroad in Baltimore, and the tracks and terminus of Camden Station, now shut down. From here, the railroad line went to Cumberland and its coal mines in 1842, and to Wheeling, West Virginia, in 1853.

canals were complemented by the Raritan River and the Morris Canal, joining Jersey City, on the Hudson River, to Phillipsburg, Easton's twin city on the New Jersey side of the Delaware River. The Morris Canal was used between 1830 and 1920.

The Delaware & Hudson Canal is remembered today thanks to the preservation of the aqueduct to which Robert M. Vogel, one of the curators of the Smithsonian Institution, devoted a key study in 1971. In 1847–50, at the start of his career, John A. Roebling, who was born in Saxonburg, Pennsylvania, and later designed the Brooklyn Bridge, built four suspension bridges that allowed the canal to pass over the Delaware River and its tributary, the Lackawaxen, which provided access to the coal mines of Lackawanna, in the Moosic Mountains. The canal, which had been designed in 1823 by Benjamin Wright, chief engineer of the Erie Canal, was then built between 1825 and 1829. In the beginning, it had only a very modest clearance (a depth of four feet, a breadth of twenty-eight feet at water level), allowing passage only to boats loaded with twenty tons of coal or less. As a result, the canal was periodically widened, increasing its capacity to 145 tons by 1852. In 1844–45, Roebling had already built a similar aqueduct in Pittsburgh for crossing the Monongahela via the Pennsylvania Canal, for which he was the engineer. His reputation as a specialized manufacturer of metal cables was already established: the metal strands were not joined by torsion, but placed parallel to one another and compressed into a cylindrical shape, then surrounded by a peripheral layer of strands over their entire circumference. The load-bearing structure of the Delaware and Lackawaxen aqueduct relied on masonry supports holding four spans. This bridge, which eliminated the need to transship a large quantity of cargo, remained in service until 1898. It then became private property; purchased by a timber dealer, it was transformed into a road bridge, and then became a toll bridge in 1900. Purchased by the National Park Service in 1980, the bridge was listed as a national historic landmark in 1986 and was reopened to one lane of automobile traffic in the same year.

RAILROADS

Despite the massive shrinkage of the railroad transportation system in the United States over the last half century—as demonstrated by the miles of tracks buried under weeds or by the defunct engines and train cars rusting away on side tracks or in engine sheds—American railroads have not completely lost the components of their architectural heritage: the railway stations, the locomotive maintenance shops, and the storage facilities located near the railway.

In the early years of the twentieth century, in the large metropolises of the country, train stations began to display a monumental character charged with symbolism. The architecture glorified a tool of transportation and communication that had been partly responsible for unifying the nation and making it economically prosperous; celebrated, in the style of all large public buildings, a sense of national greatness; and enhanced the image of the city with its monumental presence and symbolic gate, which announced the city's identity.

From the Atlantic Ocean to the Midwest, from New York to St. Louis, these stations have been restored over the last two decades, in conjunction with the project of restoring, at least in part, the rail network itself and of modernizing its operation. That undertaking has been part of Amtrak's development program since the 1970s. The trend in favor of rehabilitation reversed a tendency that had threatened the most glorious monuments ever since the destruction of Pennsylvania Station in Manhattan after only a few decades of existence. Pennsylvania Station, which had been the terminus of the Pennsylvania Railroad, was built when the railroad had finally penetrated New York after the long-delayed boring of a tunnel under the Hudson River. Will the station, replaced by an underground terminal that is proving inadequate to the needs of traffic, ever be rebuilt? A short distance to the west is New York's central post office—also completely unsuited to present-day needs—a sort of enormous classical temple with inscriptions praising the audacity of those who, in every sort of weather, ensure the coast-to-coast delivery of mail. The post office and the now-demolished station formed a monumental, neoclassical pair, a brilliant expression of urbanism. Today, plans to convert the post office into a new Penn Station are under consideration.

The same neoclassical style is also found, with variations in scale, along the Washington–New York corridor: notably at 30th Street Station in Philadelphia and at Penn Station in Baltimore. Among the grander examples of stations designed in the style of the Ecole des Beaux-Arts, which had a great influence on American architecture around the turn of the twentieth century, are Washington's Union Station, built in 1907 by the architect Daniel Burnham, and, to an even greater degree, New York's Grand Central Station.

The New York Central Railroad Company's first train station in Manhattan dated from 1869 and was expanded by the architect Cass Gilbert in 1898. This was a time when the city, having annexed Brooklyn, The Bronx, Queens, and Staten Island, had more than 3 million residents and was asserting itself as the nation's capital of trade and communications. In 1903, a new station was designed by the engineer William Wilgus and the architects Warren and Wetmore; it was inaugurated in 1913. The building was as grandiose on the inside, with its vast barrel-vaulted hall, as it was on the outside, with its arched doorways, double columns, and exuberant sculptures. Its exuberance was reminiscent of the Paris Opera or the Gare d'Orsay. Grand Central Station managed to be impressive, despite being squeezed into the fabric of the city's gridded streets. It escaped the barbaric intentions of the railroad's owners, who, in the mid-1950s, considered demolishing it and replacing it with a giant office tower, the first plans for which were produced by the architect I. M. Pei. The station was saved thanks to the prompt mobilization of architects, politicians, and preservationists who considered it a national treasure. However, the protestations could not stop the construction of the Pan Am (now Met Life) Building, a skyscraper designed by Walter Gropius and Pietro Beluschi (1963), which abuts and looms over the station.

Grand Central Station was not only an architectural achievement on a grand scale but also a technical masterpiece. Extending seven levels below ground and with rail lines heading north under Park Avenue, it connects to all the transportation networks in the city.

The placement of the maintenance shops and locomotive roundhouses close to the stations was commonplace, dating back to the era of steam power, prior to the shift to diesel. Remarkable specimens of these facilities survive, the legacy of the pioneering Baltimore & Ohio Railroad, which in about 1830 shifted from horse-drawn trains to trains with steam locomotives. The company owed its success to the fact that it was able to build and repair all its own rolling stock (which included, notably, hundreds of locomotives), not to mention dozens of bridges. In Baltimore, the Mount Clare shops, very close to the roundhouse, were among the largest in the world in the mid-nineteenth century. The roundhouse itself, built by the architect E. Francis Baldwin, does not date from the early history of the company, but from 1883–84; at that time, the twenty-two-sided polygonal structure was the largest "circular" industrial building in the world (about 230 feet in diameter). It is of an extraordinary quality, with brick walls concealing the wrought-iron columns and frame that support the inside of the roof, the ridge turret, and the dome. The twenty-two radial tracks and the turntable, which was used until 1953 for passenger-car construction and repair, have since been adapted to display the B&O Railroad museum collection.

The B&O played an important role in the history of Baltimore and in the railroad heritage of the United States. In 1827, the prominent citizens of that port city, understanding that it was poorly situated geographically in the competition among several east–west waterway connections, had the foresight to opt for the method of transport then prevailing in Great Britain: the railroad. Baltimore's political leaders and major economic interests decided to develop a railroad link to Wheeling, on the Ohio River. They entrusted the project to a company recognized by the states of Pennsylvania, Maryland, and Virginia. Never before had anyone envisioned building a railway through a region covered with a thick forest and across a barrier like the Appalachians. In 1834, construction was interrupted when the line reached the Harpers Ferry pass. The railroad company and the Chesapeake & Ohio Canal Company fought over the use of that narrow strip of

Above: *A covered bridge dating from 1857 at Humpback, in Covington, Virginia. It is not known who designed this bridge, built to accommodate a toll road. It has a wood transept structure on the interior. Its arch form makes it one of a kind in the United States.*

Left: *A covered bridge in Bridgeport, California.*

Below: *A wood railroad bridge (1902–04) in Ogden-Lucin, Utah, near the major branch line of the Southern Pacific Railroad.*

Right: *A detail of the trestle support structure, which has 38,256 wood pillars supporting the deck of the bridge.*

Top: *A bridge over the Casselman River on Interstate 40, near Grantsville, Maryland. This extraordinarily elegant arch spans one of the countless waterways located along this highway, which opened between 1811 and 1818. It was the first interstate in the United States, and the first to traverse the Appalachian Mountains.*

Above: *The design of the Thomas Viaduct in Maryland, on the branch line of the B&O heading toward Washington, D.C., is characterized by a very bold curve. It was an early and lasting technological success, and is still in service for suburban and freight trains.*

Right: *Near Staunton, Virginia, the Folly Mills Creek Viaduct and its four magnificent arches date from 1874. This B&O bridge attests to the fondness of many engineers for the use of stone for this type of structure. It has not been in service since 1942.*

Above: *The Schoharie Creek Aqueduct in Tribes Hill, New York. A major achievement, this canal bridge was built between 1839 and 1841, when the Erie Canal was being widened for the first time. Nine of the fourteen masonry arches still survive.*

Opposite: *Starrucca Viaduct near Lanesboro, Pennsylvania.*

Above: *The Wheeling Bridge (1859), designed by Charles Ellet and built on the Ohio River, offers a surprising contrast between its monumental stone supporting piers and arches and the system of metal cables holding up the deck.*

Left: *A detail of the juncture of the suspension cables and one of the masonry piers of the Delaware Aqueduct (see page 114).*

Opposite: *The network of cables anchored to the top of one of the towers of the Brooklyn Bridge (1867–83) in New York. This major achievement by John, Washington, and Emily Roebling is remarkable for the strength of its masonry piers, from which a web of 1,520 suspension cables (incorporating 3,500 miles of wire) is suspended, interrupted at regular intervals by diagonal cables. The four weight-bearing cables each measure more than fifteen inches in diameter. The bridge crosses the East River, between Manhattan and Brooklyn, 275 feet above the water. Its two towers are sunk, respectively, 75 and 43 feet into the ground. They were built with the help of pressurized caissons, following procedures that caused many deaths among the workers and engineers.*

Left: *The deck of the Brooklyn Bridge.*

Below left: *The Manhattan Bridge (1910–15) spans the East River between Manhattan and Brooklyn along 1,640 feet. It supports a double deck (for road and subway traffic). Its elegant towers (Carrère & Hastings, architects) announce the triumph of steel.*

Below right: *The Verrazano Narrows Bridge in New York City, crosses the Narrows between Brooklyn and Staten Island with a single span. Its deck is 215 feet above the water, allowing ships entering and leaving the port of New York to pass underneath.*

132

land, which would make it possible to travel along the Potomac River, near its confluence with the Shenandoah River. Wheeling was not reached until 1853, but the long construction period was an opportunity to effectively solve a large number of technical problems concerning civil engineering and materials. Farther west on that same line, the roundhouse in Martinsburg, West Virginia, built in 1866 to replace an 1849 structure destroyed by the Confederate Army, displays an impressive umbrella-shaped metal framework supporting the ventilation dome that allowed the locomotive smoke to escape.

The roundhouse of Georgia Railroad's central train station in Savannah, Georgia, was destroyed in 1927; however, the shops and facilities at that starting point of the network constitute the most beautiful railroad complex surviving in the United States from the pre–Civil War period (1855). This extraordinary site, whose operations (resumed by the Southern Railway during the Great Depression) were abandoned in 1966, was in part saved from ruin and demolition thanks to the combined efforts of the HAER (which resulted in its being classified as a national historic landmark in 1978) and the municipality of Savannah. The city, being sensitive to the quality of its urban and architectural heritage, played a key preservation role by buying the land and buildings; it became interested in the old railway installation not for its value in the country's technological and industrial heritage, but for its location on the site of the Battle of Savannah (1776). The bicentennial of that historic Revolutionary War event was being celebrated at the time. The city's involvement was only the beginning of the path toward effective rehabilitation.

The presence of warehouses connected to railroads was of great significance to the history of economic growth in the United States. Hence, the landscape of the Great Plains is marked by grain elevators spread out at regular intervals along the transcontinental lines, as so many indispensable relay points in the long journey of grains and cereal resources from their production sites to large milling centers and exportation ports. Beginning in the 1880s, railroads increased wholesale and warehouse trade by a factor of ten. Warehouses bordering the major thoroughfares proliferated in the cities that served as gateways to the large agricultural regions, especially those with access to large waterways and coastal ports. The Midwestern cities sometimes possessed true warehouse districts, whose buildings were not devoid of decorative refinements, despite the austerity of the facades and the preponderance of narrow window openings (the warehouse being vulnerable to damage from light and fire).

BRIDGES BY THE THOUSANDS

"Just imagine a world without bridges!" exclaimed Henry Petroski in his *Great Bridge Builders and the Spanning of America* (1995). The artistic and civil-engineering achievements of bridge builders played an indispensable role in the progress of the country's settlement and in the construction of the road and railway systems (and even of the canal networks). As Eric DeLony notes, the country's growing and mobile population, which for generations had been confronted with the task of spanning hundreds of thousands of waterways, sometimes very deep or very wide, or of crossing marshlands, cannot help but feel a real affection for its bridges. They were a primary catalyst for unification and development, as well as a spur for the creativity of engineers and builders. The undertaking mobilized vast financial resources, not to mention human resources—entrepreneurs, technicians, and engineers with multiple areas of expertise.

American and European bridges share certain historical developments. On both sides of the Atlantic, wood and stone were used early on in the building of bridges. When attention turned to the use of modern materials—metal and concrete in their various forms—technological exchanges multiplied between Europe and the United States, and even today they rival each other in daring and creativity in the design of longer, safer bridges, with increasingly functional forms.

The United States is known for the originality of its wooden bridges, and more particularly of its covered bridges, designed to protect the roadway from snow and ice. No examples survive of covered bridges built in the eighteenth century, but numerous examples of such bridges constructed in the middle of the nineteenth century survive, such as the one in Humpback, Virginia, which dates from 1857. The state of New Hampshire, exposed to harsh winters, once had as many as four hundred covered bridges, fifty-one of which still survived in 1994. The most impressive one, the Cornish-Windsor Bridge, on the Connecticut River, has been restored. The subject of covered bridges has become so popular that, since 1995, there has even been an annual covered bridge festival in Newport, New Hampshire. Similar bridges can be found in the mountainous regions of California: the example in Bridgeport, on a road linking San Francisco to the silver mines of western Nevada and dating from 1862, is the longest single-span covered bridge in the world.

The impressive wooden structures of railroad viaducts straddle deep valleys which, as far east as the Appalachian Mountains, might have otherwise blocked penetration into the country's interior. It was unimaginable that railroad tracks would go down one slope and up the other—they would have been too steep and too costly. Wood was also used to span shallow bodies of water, as in the case of the Ogden Lucin Bridge across the Salt Lake in Utah. In the genealogy of technologies, wooden bridges prefigured metal bridges in the use of the truss, a system of intersecting wood (and later, iron) beams, whose function was to solidify the lateral support of the bridge while preserving a certain elasticity, and to increase the span between two support pillars. The structure of the truss system could be expressed in many shapes (particularly arches and trapezoids), an opportunity for American engineers to experiment with and develop a remarkably imaginative repertoire based on formalized mathematical calculations.

Stone bridges also have a long history in the United States, which is a function of the material itself, but is also related to its technological advantages, whatever the era and despite advances in technology. Some are modest granite bridges for road traffic, such as certain bridges built for the National Road in western Maryland, the Casselman Bridge in Grantsville, for example. But

there are also large stone railroad bridges, artistic achievements that are as spectacular as the panoramic valleys they cross.

When the pioneering Baltimore & Ohio Railroad began to build its lines in 1828, an internal debate pitted its engineers against one another on the question of whether they ought to use wood, to build quickly and inexpensively—as the construction of a network throughout a country as expansive as America seemed to require—or stone, for solidity and permanence, as the experiment in building the National Road and the example of the British railroads seemed to recommend. The first solution was defended by the "mathematicians," that is, the military engineers from West Point, and applied to large public-works projects. It was the second solution that prevailed, however, on the advice of "practitioners," who had little confidence in the ability of wood frameworks to withstand the speed and weight of the train convoys.

The Carrollton Viaduct, outside Baltimore en route to Washington, built in 1829, shares with the Canton Viaduct (built over the Neponset River on the Boston–Providence line) the distinction of being the oldest railroad bridge in the United States. The Carrollton Viaduct is made of granite from the quarries near Ellicott City, and crosses the small coastal river of Gwynn Falls via a majestic Roman arch with a ninety-foot span. From 1832 to 1835, the B&O would also build one of the first multiarch railroad bridges, the Thomas Viaduct, which crosses the Patapsco River somewhat farther along the route. The largest of the company's masonry bridges (650 feet long, with eight elliptical arches), and also its last, it was executed by Benjamin H. Latrobe Jr. (1807–1878), son of the architect of the U.S. Capitol Building in Washington, and, beginning in 1842, the company's chief engineer. These two historic B&O bridges are still in use. Thus, the company inaugurated a heritage rich in successes in the field of civil engineering. Under Latrobe's leadership, the company also sought a compromise between its different schools of thought.

The Starrucca Viaduct, in northeastern Pennsylvania (Lanesboro), built in 1847–48 during a period of competition with the region's canals, spanned a deep valley with a remarkable clearance height and seventeen arches; in 1865, it attracted the attention of Jasper Francis Cropsey (1823–1900), a landscape painter who, in the tradition of the Hudson River School, celebrated the harmonious alliance between nature and human achievements.

Even though the railroad companies soon began to use iron (but without excluding the use of wood) for their bridges, as the railway lines moved farther into the country's interior, stone later made a spectacular return. Thus, in 1902 in Rockville, upstream from Harrisburg, Pennsylvania, the Pennsylvania Railroad built the longest masonry railroad bridge, replacing an earlier iron-and-steel-frame bridge; the company believed at the time that the heavy investment would be recouped by the low cost of maintenance.

Nevertheless, in the early nineteenth century, small quantities of metal had been introduced into bridge construction, used in conjunction with stone piers and porticoes in the evolution of a new technology: the suspension bridge. That technique was a particularly effective response to the challenges of the long spans that were frequently imposed by the extreme American topography. Thus, in Europe and the New World, a technology reemerged that apparently had been known for two thousand years in the high-altitude zones of the Himalayas and the Andes, and which came to the attention of the West in the seventeenth and eighteenth centuries.

To hold the deck of the bridge, chain suspension was first used, following the experiments of James Finley, a judge from Uniontown, Pennsylvania, who in 1801 built the first modern suspension bridge (about an eighty-foot span). The suspension system was anchored in masonry blocks and supported by wood-frame towers. Until his death in 1828, Finley had a following in the United States—where about twenty bridges of the same type were undertaken—as well as in England, among engineers as well known as Brown, Telford, and Brunel. Brown even formulated a vigorous condemnation of cable suspension, which he described as good only for footbridges and temporary structures. The British engineer's position found defenders among the graduates of the Ecole Polytechnique in Paris.

However, in 1830 to 1840, it was the French school of suspension bridges—exemplified by the work of engineer Marc Seguin with the construction of the Tournon Bridge over the Rhône River in 1825—that imposed the use of metal-cable suspension, finding the method superior to chains or eyebars (metal bars connected to one another via loops at either end) in withstanding stress. The competition between the different suspension systems marked a very active episode in the circulation of technologies and in scientific debates on both sides of the Atlantic; but ultimately the choice between them was a function of the production capacities of the metallurgical industries in the respective countries. Strands of cable were less expensive to manufacture and corresponded better to the capacities of less advanced industries, such as those of the United States and France. Conversely, the triumph of British technology demonstrated by the erection of the Crystal Palace in 1851, during the Great Exhibition in London, was an indication of that country's supremacy in the manufacture of large wrought- or cast-iron components for use in public works or engineering feats.

All the same, the competition among several technological models was also in keeping with the coexistence of two methodological models in Western thought: that of the engineers from the French Ecole des Ponts et Chaussées, thoroughly trained in mathematics and theoretical mechanics; and that of British civil engineers, who had an experimental mindset. It was the latter that allowed craftsmen and builders to innovate via empirical pursuits. The first of these models was deeply ingrained in the training given at the West Point military academy, to officers who were recruited to serve civilian as well as military needs, and who played a prominent role in the first large public-works enterprises (the National Road and the Baltimore & Ohio Railroad).

In any case, suspension by cables became deeply rooted in American technological culture, allowing bridges to cross increasingly greater distances. Up to the second half of the twentieth century, as records were repeatedly broken, technical, economic, aesthetic, and even political debates continued to surround the question of bridges in the United States, a subject dear to specialists as well as to a broader public.

Two names are associated with the introduction of cable-suspension bridges in the United States. The first was Charles Ellet. Born in 1810, he began as an assistant engineer in the building of the Chesapeake & Ohio Canal. At the age of twenty, he decided to take courses in Paris at the Ecole des Ponts et Chaussées. In 1842, he built his first bridge, over the Schuylkill River near Philadelphia. In 1859, he undertook construction of a bridge in Wheeling, West Virginia, on the Ohio River, spanning a length of a thousand feet between its suspension towers. This bridge was the object of a series of restorations beginning in 1983.

The second figure was John A. Roebling, the son of a German immigrant. Even though he had been educated in Berlin, he returned from Europe with the same convictions as Ellet regarding cable suspension. He too would undertake to cross the Ohio, with the Cincinnati suspension bridge in 1866. The Roebling dynasty used the extraordinary boom in bridge construction as a springboard to a national industrial enterprise. That destiny took shape with a canal suspension bridge in Pittsburgh over the Monongahela River (1845) and another for the Delaware & Hudson Canal (1847–1850), and then with a double-decker (road and rail) suspension bridge across the Niagara Gorge in 1856.

In 1848 Roebling acquired the site that the firm would occupy until it folded in the 1970s, in Chambersburg, a neighborhood of Trenton, New Jersey, along the Delaware & Raritan Canal, midway between New York and Philadelphia. For 125 years, that firm provided metal cables to be used in all sorts of technological innovations, not only in bridge construction but also in transportation, building construction, and communications. All the large suspension bridges owed a debt to the Roebling company, from the Brooklyn Bridge to the Verrazano Narrows Bridge. John A. Roebling's Sons (the founding father made his four sons partners) expanded so much that, in the 1890s and then in the early twentieth century, two other establishments were created. The second of them, Kinkora Works, was located nine miles to the south. Charles Roebling, president of the company at the

time, then designed an entire city, also called Roebling, complete with schools and all public buildings. At the end of World War I, the business had more than eight thousand employees. It had its own department of architecture and engineering, and permanent teams of masons, carpenters, and fitters. The site, though it was constantly evolving and being rebuilt, contains remarkable relics of the different eras of industrial architecture and is the object of preservation efforts.

The Brooklyn Bridge, designed by John Roebling in the late 1860s, was built by his son, Washington, between 1870 and 1883. The neighboring Manhattan Bridge dates from 1909, and was designed by a different engineer. Most of the other great bridge achievements of the twentieth century date from a later period and were the exclusive domain of a small group of ambitious European engineers who immigrated to the United States.

Othmar Ammann (1879–1965) represents the most astounding episode of American engineering as far as suspension bridges are concerned. Over half a century, there was a race to break the record for the length of a span's deck (whose enormous weight is a gauge of stability). The Verrazano Narrows Bridge, the prestigious gateway to New York Bay, reaches a length of nearly four thousand feet between two support pillars. It owes its design to improvements in the quality of steel cables and in advanced technology of modern bridges, capable of withstanding any load and any storm.

Born in Switzerland and trained at the Polytechnikum in Zurich, Ammann emigrated to the United States in 1904. His arrival in New York coincided with the rise of an intense debate around the need to provide the city with a unified transportation network of roads and bridges. Brooklyn, Manhattan, and the New Jersey cities along the Hudson River were experiencing a tremendous expansion in their industrial and commercial activity, which relied primarily on rail and river service. Without a unified transportation system, New York would not have retained its commercial dominance on the northeastern coast, nor would it have developed its role as a global economic metropolis. In particular, plans and debates had long centered on the problem of

The George Washington Bridge crosses the Hudson River and connects the states of New York and New Jersey. Note the very long access ramp required for this type of bridge. In the history of suspension bridges, this bridge was notable for doubling the length of spans previously achieved (in this case, more than three thousand feet). That achievement was made possible by an improvement in the quality of the steel and an increase by half in the strength of the cables, compared to that of the cables used for the Brooklyn Bridge.

Opposite: The suspension cables and deck of the George Washington Bridge.

Right: *The Bayonne Bridge in New Jersey incorporates a single metal-frame arch and a series of cables holding up the deck.*

Below: *The two-part Triborough Bridge in New York, linking Manhattan, The Bronx, and Queens. The upper section, which joins Manhattan and Queens, includes a center span that elevates to accommodate boat traffic.*

Above: *The Throgs Neck Bridge in New York, spanning the East River between The Bronx and Queens.*

Right: *The Golden Gate Bridge in San Francisco, California, designed by Joseph Strauss and his assistant Charles Ellis, dates from 1933–37. Its towers are masterpieces of architecture and engineering: rising to 750 feet above San Francisco Bay, they support a 4,200-foot span.*

Left: *A metal railroad bridge in Savage, Maryland, on the Little Patuxent River. Wendell Bollman's suspension bridges were often used on the B&O Railroad route between 1850 and 1875. This bridge is the first of its kind to have attracted the attention of American historians of engineering, in the late 1960s.*

Below: *This 1871 metal bridge in Riverside, Connecticut, combines the use of cast iron and wrought iron. The cross braces are of the Whipple type. It is a railroad bridge that was moved from its original site and converted into a road bridge.*

Opposite: *One of the arches of the Eads Bridge (1874) in St. Louis, Missouri. This bridge, which Eric DeLony calls "the most elegant of the bridges crossing the Mississippi," is also the first in which steel was widely used alongside wrought iron.*

Opposite: The two bridges that cross the Hudson River at Poughkeepsie, New York. Above, the older, metal-frame railroad bridge (1888) held the record for length for a single steel structure at the time of its construction. It was abandoned by Conrail in 1974 after a fire. A local organization took on the task of opening it to light railroad traffic and pedestrian use. Below, the road suspension bridge.

Right and below: *The Smithsfield Street Bridge (1883) in Pittsburgh, Pennsylvania, crosses the Monongahela River a short distance from its confluence with the Allegheny River. It is noteworthy for its lenticular design with lateral reinforcements. The bridge serves both road and streetcar traffic.*

Above: *A metal-frame (cantilever) railroad bridge above the Niagara River, constructed with steel provided by Bethlehem Steel Company.*

Right: *A double elevated-lift bridge in the port city of Newark, New Jersey.*

Opposite, top left: *An elevated-lift railroad bridge in Massachusetts.*

Opposite, top right: *The Westinghouse Bridge in Pennsylvania provides proof that concrete can rival steel in elegance and lightness, while serving the same function.*

Opposite, bottom: *The Aslea Bay Bridge in Waldport, Oregon is one of a number of engineering feats located along Oregon's shipping route. This 1936 concrete bridge attests both to the success of the technology of prestressed concrete, perfected by the engineer Eugène Freyssinet, and to the relative fragility of that material—the bridge later had to be rebuilt.*

spanning the Hudson and on the point best suited for a bridge to be built. The Regional Plan Association was created in 1914 to address these issues. In 1929, it imposed a plan for highway connections destined to give the New York urban area its modern structure and appearance, and intended to provide a new system of commuting between home and work that made it possible to relieve congestion in the city.

Ammann first collaborated with the engineer Gustav Lindenthal. Together they drafted an ambitious plan, in 1920, to span the Hudson River at Fifty-seventh Street, via a bridge that would have included twelve train tracks and sixteen lanes of automobile traffic. The plan truly expressed their dreams, as emigrants to the United States, to one day be able to realize artistic achievements on a scale inconceivable in Europe. But success came only later, when, as chief engineer for the newly conceived Port Authority of New York and New Jersey, Ammann collaborated with Robert Moses, the agency's administrator, and with the engineer Leon Moisseif. From then on, one achievement followed another. In 1931, a first masterpiece, the construction of the George Washington Bridge, which finally made possible a surface crossing of the Hudson, led to a controversy regarding whether the steel framework of its main towers ought to be sheathed in concrete and stone, or rather left exposed. For both economic and aesthetic reasons, the second solution was adopted. The Bayonne Bridge was built the same year, linking Staten Island and Bayonne, New Jersey. Shortly after, in 1936, the Triborough Bridge—a complex structure combining a vertical-lift bridge, a viaduct, and a suspension bridge—was erected to link Manhattan, The Bronx, and Queens. Then came the Whitestone Bridge in 1939 and the Throgs Neck Bridge in 1961, both joining The Bronx and Queens; and, finally, the last large bridge to be built in New York, the Verrazano Narrows Bridge in 1964, spanning the Narrows between Brooklyn and Staten Island.

The third-longest suspension bridge in the world, after the bridge spanning the Humber estuary in England and that linking Shikoku to Honshu in Japan, the Verrazano Narrows Bridge definitively put an end to the controversy spurred by the collapse of the Tacoma Narrows Bridge in Washington, designed by Leon Moisseif, an accident that occurred during a moderate storm only four months after the bridge was opened.

On that occasion, newspapers such as the *New York Times* and the *Engineering News Record* had essentially orchestrated the debate pitting supporters of cantilever bridges (a technique combining a central open span and strong frameworks resting on piers at either end), which still appeared more reassuringly rigid and stable, and proponents of suspension bridges. But experts on suspension bridges proved to be well organized. David Steinmann, a former assistant to Lindenthal who became the world expert on these wind-resistant bridges and himself the builder of four hundred structures—among them a superb bridge spanning the Straits of Mackinac in Michigan, between Lake Huron and Lake Michigan—founded the National Society of Professional Engineers.

Outside New York during the interwar period, two major artistic achievements illustrated the same techniques: the Ambassador Bridge (1929), which joined Detroit, Michigan, and Windsor, Canada; and the Golden Gate Bridge (1937) across San Francisco Bay, designed by Joseph Strauss.

In recounting the achievements in American bridges, it would be wrong to focus exclusively on the technology of suspension bridges. Everyday reality in nineteenth-century America called for other solutions. Metal bridges were used to support a homogeneous network of roads and railroads, and it was their technology that truly mobilized the creative capacities of American engineering applied to this field. Bridges by the thousands were built of cast and wrought iron between 1840 and 1880, before the use of steel prevailed. The fact that only a few dozen of these reliable—and often modest—structures survive should not diminish the historical importance of their role in the struggle to overcome some of the physical obstacles posed in the expansion of the nation. These metal bridges made it possible to build a network of railroads, for they did not possess the performance limitations that wood displayed in bridge construction. All the same, many of the bridges of this period combined the use of wood and iron in their construction. It took the public a certain amount of time to rally behind cast iron, wrought iron, and steel, since generally there was a poor perception of their respective qualities in terms of compression and stress resistance. In any case, these materials were infinitely superior to wood by virtue of their incombustibility, their resistance to deterioration, and their ability to support heavy loads.

The proliferation of metal bridges was made possible through the efforts of various proponents. The West Point military academy, founded in New York in 1802, played a formative role. One of its first directors, Sylvanus Thayer, decided in 1817 to model the curriculum on that of the Ecole Polytechnique in Paris. During a trip to Europe, he visited the military schools and returned with Polytechnique graduate Claudius Crozet, named professor of civil engineering at West Point. Crozet won acceptance for scientific training with a mathematical basis and introduced the ideas and concepts of French engineering into the manuals and courses. For half a century, engineers with that training played an essential role in the construction of American transportation networks (roads, canals, and railroads), to which they applied their theoretical knowledge and their rigorous mathematical calculations. Every military engineer who came out of that school was qualified to assume the duties of a civil engineer. Thus, Colonel Stephen Harriman Long (1784–1864), in his capacity as engineer and topographer, was employed by the B&O Railroad in its infancy; he also made a name for himself with a model of truss valued for its simplicity and the ease of its assembly. The first arch bridge made entirely of iron, built in 1839, was Dunlap Creek Bridge, in Brownsville, Pennsylvania, which was erected as part of the famous National Road. It was designed by Captain Richard Delafield, a general engineer who had built fortifications and rectified currents on segments of the Ohio and Mississippi Rivers.

All the same, artistic achievements in bridge building were also executed by civil engineers without college degrees, or by graduates of schools other than West Point, and their role became more important beginning in the mid-nineteenth century.

The increasingly widespread use of iron for all purposes in bridge construction, beginning in the 1840s, owes a great deal to Squire Whipple. A university graduate, he participated in work on the Erie Canal and on the B&O Railroad before publishing, in 1847, the first treatise on bridge construction and a mathematical analysis of overlapping-beam frameworks, of which he had built original models. Latrobe's collaborators at the B&O Railroad, such as Wendel Bollmann, a former pharmacist from Baltimore, and Albert Fink, a graduate of the technical university in Darmstadt, played a decisive role in promoting the use of metal bridges for crossing the Appalachians and in developing new models of trusses. The Bollmann truss was tried out for the first time in 1849, on a branch line serving the textile factory in Savage, Maryland. At that site the only surviving model of this technique has since been reassembled, an example that is, in fact, about twenty years newer.

Furthermore, bridge construction at the local level was often the expression of an artisanal tradition and pragmatism carried on by smiths, millwrights, and mechanics who manufactured or repaired farm equipment, men who worked in family businesses and lived by practical experience.

Finally, in the second half of the nineteenth century, firms specializing in bridge construction multiplied (there would be 190 in 1900). Employing the services of engineers, they offered a catalog of prefabricated and standardized metal components, deliverable anywhere in the United States by railroad, and even exported to the world market. Among the most famous of these are the Keystone in Pittsburgh and the Phoenix Bridge Works in the Schuylkill Valley, near Philadelphia. The latter, created in 1790, became famous in the early nineteenth century for its wooden bridges, before moving to the forefront of iron-and-steel production techniques.

It was at the Phoenix firm that engineer John Fritz perfected his revolutionary rolling process for the manufacture of rails, and where the engineer Samuel Reeves patented the Phoenix pillar (1862) and published the first printed specifications for bridge construction (1864). In 1900, Phoenix managed

Above: *The Imperial Warehouse in Brooklyn, New York, shows the architectural influence of mid-nineteenth-century British docks.*

Right: *Warehouses on Manhattan's West Side.*

Opposite, top: *The Great Northern Elevator in Buffalo, New York.*

Opposite, bottom left: *Steel sheets were bolted together to form the interior walls of a metal "cell" or compartment of the Great Northern Elevator.*

Opposite, bottom right: *A "marine leg" is thrust into the hold of a ship to suck out the grain and transport it to the top of the elevator.*

Above: *The Concrete-Central Elevator in Buffalo, New York. The metal armature of the grain transportation system is visible on the facade.*

Right: *The interior of the ground floor of a concrete elevator, the Cargill Superior Elevator in Buffalo. The structure is reinforced by columns with flared capitals, designed to support the enormous load of the thousands of tons of grain poured into the cells.*

to avoid the American Bridge Company's absorption of twenty-four similar firms, under the aegis of John Pierpont Morgan, who was a powerful driving force behind the trend toward consolidation of the American iron, steel, and metallurgy industries. Bollmann, a former employee of the B&O Railroad, also created his own company at that time, the Patapsco Bridge and Iron Works in Baltimore.

Thus, as Eric DeLony notes, the history of American bridges illustrates the interconnectedness of numerous scientific, socioeconomic, political, and artistic factors: new technologies, theories regarding the resistance of different materials, manufacturing and commercial strategies, clashes between professionalism and practical expertise, the settlement of the West, the aesthetics of bridges, and so on—in short, an intersection open to multiple cultural analyses. However, one essential factor eventually took precedence in the development of American bridges: the rapid replacement of one metal with another that occurred during the nineteenth century.

Beginning in the late eighteenth century, there was a growing tendency toward the massive production of wood-fueled, then coke-fueled, cast iron, and of puddled, rolled, and wrought iron. Because of their technical capacities and relatively low cost, these products passed for miracle materials in the field of civil engineering. Cast and wrought iron, however, had rigorously distinct and complementary qualities. Furthermore, the differences in their potential use had to be respected: cast iron for the parts of engineering projects that had to withstand strong compression, wrought iron for those that were primarily subject to stress. Errors in combining one material with the other could produce catastrophes. In the United States, one of the most spectacular railway disasters was the collapse of the Ashtabula Bridge in Ohio in 1876: this 1865 bridge plunged into the water, carrying seventy-six people to their deaths. A report of the American Society of Civil Engineers recommended shifting to the construction of bridges made entirely of riveted wrought iron. Cast iron could break without warning. Its composition was not always homogeneous: if its degasification was not well supervised, it could be riddled with holes. It was nonetheless used for girders and pillars over a long period of time. The use of wrought iron dropped off more slowly.

With the spread of the Bessemer process for the manufacture of steel, that metal gradually gained ground, and, in the 1880s, in addition to its uses in naval and building construction, it became the chief material in the construction of railway bridges. It responded well to the increase in the weight of locomotives and freight convoys.

The success of riveted steel was illustrated by an important episode in the conquest of the American continent by engineers: the spanning of the Mississippi River, an obstacle previously reputed to be insurmountable (except by boat). In 1874, the engineer John Buchanan Eads, who also sought to build a system of jetties at the mouth of the river, built at Saint Louis a monumental triple-arch bridge, with each arch about 550 feet long. Soon, an indispensable collaboration was established between engineers and steel makers such as Andrew Carnegie and Paul Mellon. The second bridge over the Mississippi, built in Memphis in 1892, required the consumption of a ton of steel per foot. The large metal railway viaducts, such as the one in the Kinzua Creek Valley, in northwestern Pennsylvania, on the route of the Erie Railroad (1900), also required massive quantities of steel.

Among the major engineers of the period was Theodore Cooper, a specialist in cantilever railroad bridges. Aware of accidents that had occurred in Europe (especially the collapse of the Firth of Tay Bridge in Scotland in 1879, and the construction nearby of the new Forth Bridge), Cooper was the author of tables that specified loads for the construction of railroad structures, specifications that remain in force today.

Gustav Lindenthal, born in Moravia and trained in Germany before emigrating to the United States, began his professional career in Pittsburgh, where he executed the plans for the Smithfield Street Bridge, one of the most interesting structures ever patented in the United States. It is called *lenticular*, because of the shape of the reinforcements of the trellis framework. The bridge was recently renovated, with its original style respected.

Lindenthal then went to New York, where he designed many large road and railway bridges, including, in 1909, the Queensborough Bridge spanning the East River. His masterpiece, in collaboration with Othmar Ammann, dates from 1917: it was the Hell's Gate Bridge over the East River, between Queens and The Bronx. Distinguished by its beautiful steel arches, it was the last railroad bridge to be built in the New York metropolitan area.

Finally, bridge building in the United States benefited greatly from a knowledge of reinforced-concrete construction. Following World War II, St. Paul and Minneapolis in particular constituted a test laboratory for concrete-bridge technology: six such bridges were built there between 1918 and 1929, including the Cappelen Memorial Bridge (1919–23), designed by the engineers Cappelen, Turner, and Wheeler, which crossed the Mississippi River between two steep banks, allowing the clearance needed for river traffic.

PORT FACILITIES

Throughout the world, the preservation of what remains of the technological and architectural heritage of ports is currently on the agenda. Unfortunately, that often monumental heritage has suffered terribly from the revolution in methods of shipping, the relocation of major infrastructures, and the voracity with which economic interests of all sorts have seized the obsolete waterfront areas, exploiting the desire of many large cities to regain the use of these areas for housing or recreation. The United States is no exception to this general trend. The Upper Bay in New York, navigated mainly by pleasure crafts, tour boats, and ferries, serves as evidence of this movement. With the exception of a few operations in Brooklyn, the New York port is no longer located in New York: it is now in Newark and Bayonne, New Jersey. And yet, the geography of the United States is such that, in the eastern half of the country, the sea penetrates deeply inland via its estuaries, extended by navigable rivers over hundreds of miles, and even into the Great Lakes, which serve as an interior sea. From New York, the great gateway to the world, to the intermediate storage facilities of Albany and Buffalo, the port is still present, as the silhouette of a freighter, an ore ship, or a tanker rises incongruously from inland regions.

· Historically, the functions of the ports were not limited to receiving and servicing boats. (Of the first function, only defunct piers remain, and the second function is now handled by a small number of specialized companies.) For a long time, port activities entailed a great deal of loading and unloading, as well as storage. Only the debris of the equipment formerly used to move goods has survived; in contrast, the storage function has proved more resistant. Some large port locations possessed shipyards and arsenals, and, as a result, have preserved the docks and the actual industrial complexes linked to them. Finally, the major ports did not treat only raw materials, and they did not simply load crates and sacks: they also moved human beings during massive waves of immigration.

Warehouses became an integral part of the modern port system in Europe, beginning with a model perfected in England in the nineteenth century and imitated in Marseilles and Hamburg. The United States, however, rarely adopted the European model, despite the efficiency of the construction methods, which guaranteed excellent protection against the spread of fire (a major concern of wholesalers). In Europe, the pioneering achievement in port warehouses was Albert Dock in Liverpool (1846), designed by the architect Jesse Hartley. A U.S. Congressional commission visited the site to admire its solid masonry construction and compartmentalized design, factors which made it resistant to loads and to fire. There is a modest replica of the Albert Dock architecture in the oldest of the New York warehouses, the Imperial Warehouse in Brooklyn, which is located on the East River near the Brooklyn and Manhattan bridges. Later, on the west side of Manhattan along the Hudson River, the Terminal Warehouse Company built twenty-five warehouses that were linked via an internal railroad tunnel.

In contrast to their European counterparts, the American ports, displaying their domination of the world grain market, were outfitted with batteries of grain elevators virtually without

Above: *The Thames Tow Boats Shipyard in New London, Connecticut, from a lithograph (c. 1903). The shipyard and the river it serves are named after the Thames River in London. This illustration faithfully reflects what a shipyard was like in the early twentieth century. It was notable for its marine railways: boats being repaired were winched onto land by steam engines.*

Left: *Buildings dating from the colonial period on Boston's wharf.*

Opposite, top: *The New London shipyards as they appear today.*

Opposite, bottom: *A commercial building in the old port of Boston.*

Top: *The new and old ferry terminals (left and right, respectively) at the southern tip of Manhattan, serving passenger traffic to and from Staten Island.*

Above, left and right: *The main building on Ellis Island in New York Bay, where immigrants entering the country were processed. It is now a museum of immigration.*

equal. The prototype of the grain elevator was designed in 1843 by Joseph Dart (1799–1879), a merchant from Buffalo, New York, in partnership with the engineer Robert Dunbar (1812–1890). At that time the docks in Buffalo—an interior seaport—were no longer able to accommodate the abundant grain coming from the West. That first innovative grain elevator and others like it, made of wood, burned down during the Civil War, perhaps as a result of arson. Dunbar was also responsible for the unloading device known as the *marine leg,* a conveyer that was lowered into the hold of the ship. Since pneumatic compression was still unknown, the grain was lifted in a sort of steam-powered bucket conveyor, which, using a technical system adapted from Oliver Evans's milling operation, carried it to the top of the grain elevator. This system was a revolutionary improvement, compared to the times when porters carried sacks on their backs from the boat up to the dock, and from the dock to the storage site. Automation of grain handling occurred more easily in the United States than in Europe, given the history of ports such as Marseilles. In the United States, there was no specialization of work such as that asserted by the porters in Marseilles, for example, who belonged to different guilds depending on the work site and the merchandise they handled, and who were organized according to a hierarchy that did not exist in America. The difference between Europe and the United States is also no doubt a question of the organization of domestic and foreign trade, and of the nature of the merchandise.

In reality, the grain elevator was not a product of port technology, but the result of an organization of long-distance overland trade that was particular to the mode of settlement and development in North America. The grain elevators multiplied along the railroad lines and the large inland waterways in accordance with a system whereby crops were collected locally, then stored in volume at departure points for distant destinations or concentrated at central locations to be redistributed to the processing industries. Thus, the elevators were linked to milling operations as well as wholesale trade. The small grain elevators of the Great Plains were spaced three to fifteen miles apart, depend-

ing on whether they were in a relatively populated state such as Kansas, or a sparsely populated one, such as North Dakota. In contrast, the grain elevators in the large urban centers and ports were grouped into complexes of units spread out over hundreds of yards (at one thousand yards, the longest battery of grain elevators in the world was located in Hutchinson, Texas).

The first grain elevators were made of wood and, therefore, vulnerable to fire. Even covered with metal on the exterior, they lasted barely more than a decade on average. Toward the end of the nineteenth century, the high cost of insurance premiums under such conditions led to experimentation with other materials. All the same, the wood elevator was very popular in rural areas: economical and easy to build, it was similar in its architecture to barns and farmhouses. One of the last survivors of that generation, located in a city, is the Shoreham Elevator (1894) in Minneapolis. In 1988, the Society for Industrial Archeology lamented the destruction of an 1884 wood elevator, located in Oconomowoc, a small rural town in Wisconsin. It had been used to collect grain from the surrounding regions for the grain merchants William & Thompson, who then loaded it onto the Chicago-Milwaukee & Saint Paul Railroad.

From the late nineteenth century to about 1915, builders experimented with brick, tile, and especially steel for grain elevators. Max Foltz, a major bridge and railroad construction engineer working for the Great Northern Railway, chose steel for building giant elevators in the ports of Duluth, West Superior, and Buffalo. Nevertheless, the metal was relatively expensive and vulnerable to rust, and it had a low capacity for heat insulation, a problem in regions accustomed to extreme temperatures.

By 1915, concrete had already been established as the material of choice for elevator construction in urban areas. Concrete, an economical and durable material, was resistant to both fire and the heavy loads exerted on the inner walls of the elevator when filled with large quantities of grain. It behaved like a liquid when poured (hence the use of the cylindrical shape), was satisfactory in terms of heat insulation, and guaranteed extraordinary longevity. Elevators were built of concrete until quite recently, as in the example erected in Montreal in 1979. Concrete elevators have now become obsolete from a technological standpoint; in the last generation of structures used for grain storage, vast rectangular-shaped metal hangars have appeared, which also entail very different loading and transport procedures.

The concrete elevator originated in Minneapolis in 1899; it was built for Frank H. Peavey, a major international grain dealer. That prototype, destined to spread throughout the world, has been classified as a national historic monument; it is the pride of the city's population, many of whom are unaware of its considerable technological importance. The industrial complex of the Washburn-Crosby Company (which later became General Mills), built in the following years, includes not only grain elevators but also flour mills, warehouses, and power stations.

Between 1903 and 1909, the first complex of concrete elevators was erected in Buffalo. These structures were cited by Walter Gropius in 1913, and later by Le Corbusier, in their recommendations to twentieth-century architects to return to the use of simple geometrical forms. There were as many as fifty elevators in operation in Buffalo, serving as storage for grain in transit. In 1943, the city was the foremost grain port in the world, and subsequently passed Minneapolis as the foremost center for flour production. In 1958, the opening of the St. Lawrence Seaway and the elimination of special train fares to New York dealt Buffalo's port operations a fatal blow by changing the geography of continental traffic. In 1980, trade was limited to the demands of the needs of local flour mills; and in 1986, only four elevators survived along the Buffalo River. Duluth, a port directly across from Buffalo at the west end of the Great Lakes system, has an even larger stock of elevators, which are just as varied but less well known than those in which Minneapolis and Buffalo once took such pride.

The modern elevator belongs to a remarkable chapter of technology, and its complexity is often overshadowed by the attention paid to its architectural aesthetics. In fact, the grain elevator is much more akin to a very large machine operating outdoors than to a mere building for industrial use. Vertical and horizontal circulation—filling and emptying—weighing, sorting, and cleaning of the grain all occurred on the top story and in the storage cells. The complex shapes of the internal chambers cannot be discerned from the outside; their forms were dictated by the concern to economize on space as much as possible.

Evidence of the former commercial activity of the country's ports has become the object of documentation and preservation campaigns. Such is the case with the old port of Boston, which still contains a few landmarks evoking its appearance at the end of the colonial period and the early years of the republic, and with the small Thames Tow Boats Shipyard in New London, Connecticut, which dates from the early twentieth century and was managed by a wholesale coal merchant. Many of its buildings and a good part of its equipment are still intact.

Baltimore retains a few of the buildings most representative of a large nineteenth-century American port—in fact, one still very active in the twentieth century. That is because Baltimore encapsulates the many phases of economic development in the United States, a history in which the city has not always been given the place it deserves. Due to the general decline in the grain trade on the country's east coast, only one grain elevator, that of the old Indiana Grains Cooperative, survives in Baltimore to mark its pioneering role in the exportation of flour beginning in the eighteenth century. The city's ascension began in 1840–50, when it bravely took the initiative in building the railroad equipment needed to launch a major line penetrating the West. This development made it possible for Baltimore to maintain its role as an Atlantic coast outlet for the plains states, supplanting New Orleans and competing with New York. As witnesses to its rich industrial heritage, Camden Station (1857–65) has been preserved and restored, along with the vast eight-story Eastern Warehouse (1899–1904) next to it, which could accommodate a load equivalent to that of one thousand railroad cars. The B&O, and later the Pennsylvania Railroad, controlled large flows of both immigrants and merchandise, directly connecting the rail lines to the docks. This led to the construction of a number of warehouses serving dozens of industrial enterprises nearby. The port of Baltimore also benefited from the potential for extending its grasp along the great length of coastline of the Chesapeake Bay, well beyond the original sites of Inner Harbor and Fells Point. Thus, in the late nineteenth century and into the twentieth century, the vast shipyards of Sparrows Point and Fairfield were developed outside the city. These shipyards were linked to the Bethlehem Steel Company beginning in 1916, and from them the famous Liberty Ships (twenty-two hundred of them) and the Victory Ships emerged.

Finally, between the tip of Manhattan and New Jersey is a historically significant site that involved the transportation of people, not a place indirectly linked to the country's industrial heritage, since immigration was a catalyst in the unprecedented economic growth of the nation and made an enormous contribution to the acceleration of industry. Ellis Island and its buildings was the headquarters of the Immigration Service between January 1, 1892, and 1924, the period of mass immigration. It is

estimated that more than 16 million immigrants passed through its checkpoints before being allowed to enter the gateway to America. The main hall resembles a large train station, while various adjoining buildings were used for hospital facilities, offices, and detention areas. The Ellis Island buildings, reconstructed in 1900 after serving various other purposes, were closed in 1954, declared a national historic monument in 1965 along with the nearby Statue of Liberty, and again closed for renovation between 1984 and 1990. The main hall on the island is now open to the public as a museum, accessible by ferry.

The Upper New York Bay is also traversed by ferries linking Manhattan to Staten Island, and smaller ferries now take passengers to and from Manhattan from New Jersey. One ferry station is the former Jersey City railway station on the Hudson River waterfront. It keeps alive the memory of the historic modes of transportation and commerce between New York City and the country's interior.

CHAPTER 4

Harnessing Natural Resources

Like the conquest of the West, the 1849 gold rush was immortalized in American film. These popular images contributed toward shaping the worldwide reputation of the United States as the foremost economic power. However, that power was not established exclusively on precious metals or on agricultural products extracted from the virgin territories of the West.

Three geographical areas offered up the riches of their subsoil—coal, copper ore, and iron ore—to the country's industrialization process. These resources were exploited in a manner that sometimes caused environmental devastation. In the second half of the twentieth century, these regions began to decline and were subsequently abandoned. At issue were the Appalachian Mountains, the Great Lakes region, and the northern part of the Rocky Mountains, which, one by one, had secured the country's position as arbiter of the world market in raw materials.

UPPER MICHIGAN: COPPER AND IRON

A few years ago, the American Society for Industrial Archeology left Washington, D.C., and moved to Houghton, Michigan, near the Michigan Institute of Technology, formerly the Michigan Mining School, established in 1885 to serve as a research laboratory for the surrounding mines. It even held its annual congress there in 1997. That new location, though remote, was nonetheless meaningful since the city of Houghton was located on the Keweenaw peninsula (a narrow strip of land extending nearly seventy miles into the waters of Lake Superior), in the heart of an old mining district of premier importance.

Five thousand years earlier, the Native American populations had already been extracting, working, and trading copper throughout the North American continent. To protect the early miners against the Indians in this district, an outpost of the U.S.

Little Rock Dam in the San Gabriel Mountains (outside Los Angeles). The "slump block" concrete gives these powerful buttresses a sculptural look.

Army was created in 1844 at Fort Wilkins, just as the first frontiersmen were arriving from the East. In nearby Hancock, the Quincy Mining Company, beginning in 1846, exploited one of the largest copper mines in the world, distributing consistently high dividends from 1868 to 1920. The copper district's first sites broke records in production from the 1880s until World War I, before incurring costs associated with moving operations ever farther underground. The Quincy Mine was closed in 1931, but it reopened in 1937 as a result of the demand accompanying the approach of World War II. It has been closed since 1945, and currently represents a major heritage site.

At the height of its production in the early twentieth century, the Keweenaw peninsula employed between fifteen and eighteen thousand workers. Around Lake Portage, in the area where both the Quincy Mining Company and the Copper Range Company (active from 1899 to 1976) were operating, several company towns were developed, a few of which are well preserved: Painesdale, Coppertown, and Calumet. In the last town, the Calumet & Hecla Company built a vaudeville theater (one of the best preserved in the United States), a hospital, and a public library. From 1840 to 1920, Quincy, for its part, sought to stabilize its labor force by promoting family homes: the unmarried worker did not inspire confidence, being by definition much more mobile and representing a "volatile" workforce, always ready to change company, trade, or location. And, in relatively vacant and inhospitable regions such as those of the new mining district, stable employment took on crucial importance. In Europe, the history of the iron mines in the north of Lorraine in the second half of the nineteenth century provides a good illustration of similar concerns, despite the difference in context. Quincy perfected four home models, but it is noteworthy that each of them encountered hostile reactions from the workers. Here is a rare example of a business whose social-control policy did not achieve its objectives. Yet, that negative reaction occurred during an acute housing shortage in the region. Few examples could be found of such a negative attitude in the European history of management-furnished workers' housing.

Since the end of the nineteenth century, landscape architects with national reputations have exercised their talents in the copper region, as designers of company towns. Such was the case for Warren H. Manning (1860–1938), who had done his apprenticeship in the offices of Frederick Law Olmsted, the creator of the large city parks in New York and Boston. Over a period of thirty-five years, the firm Manning created in 1896 studied about one hundred projects for the region of Upper Michigan, where its most important clients were Calumet & Hecla (copper) and Cleveland Cliffs (iron). Its major achievements were the model city of Gwynn (1906) and the large public park in Calumet (1919).

Sandy Noyes, an American art photographer specializing in industrial archaeology, describes how, in 1997, he perceived the region's landscape, today an enormous industrial wasteland: "Beyond Houghton, the population of the peninsula fell to almost zero. I ventured to the far tip of the peninsula, to the city of Bête-Grise [Gray Beast], so named by the French Canadians, and found only a single house and a beach in its savage state. Along the way, I passed a ghost town, the former mining town of Central, which looked just like a set in the heart of Nevada, plus trees. In general, the relics from the age of the mining economy are becoming scarce: a blast furnace and the foundation of a forge, hardly more than five mine headframes, two receiver's offices, many reminders of the residential architecture and still-occupied workers' quarters. All the rest is underground: eleven thousand miles of galleries." The preservation of the heritage of the copper mining industry is nevertheless part of the efforts of the Keweenaw National Historical Park.

Along with the exploitation of copper ore, iron ore operations had begun in 1844, on the east side of Lake Superior, near Marquette, at the instigation of a group of Michigan capitalists who founded the Jackson Mining Company. In 1848, an attempt to process the ore on site at the Carp River Forge ended in failure: most of the mine owners decided henceforth to send their ore to the blast furnaces in Pennsylvania, and, later, to the Midwest. The Marquette Iron Range is still in production; the Tilden Taconite Mine & Mill has worked a large open-pit mine since 1973.

In that hilly region, evidence of the workers' quarters survives in the small towns of Negaunee and Ishpeming. The Michigan Iron Industry Museum is located in Negaunee. Ishpeming contains the best-preserved site of underground mining in the region, the Cliffs Shaft Mine, from which 32 million tons of ore were extracted between 1848 and 1967. Two shafts, built in 1919 by the architect George W. Maher, were closed down in 1955 but have fortunately been preserved; they still display their neo-Egyptian masonry lagging.

In the second half of the nineteenth century, the search to find new sources of iron ore continued. In the 1880s, deposits were discovered in Gogebic Lake in Michigan, and in 1887, in Menominee, Wisconsin, near Lake Michigan. These discoveries came just in time to supplant the Pennsylvania iron mines, which by then were completely inadequate to satisfy the needs of industry. In 1893, the Lake Superior Mining Institute was established in Menominee, with the goal of fostering an exchange of technological information among all the copper- and iron-mine engineers of the region. The institute held its annual conference at a different mining site every year, organizing its visit to the mines through the use of a special train, aboard which participants slept and took their meals.

A major event in the late nineteenth century was to bestow worldwide economic importance to the Lake Superior region. This was the 1891 discovery by the Merritt brothers of the Mesabi Range deposit in Minnesota, fifty miles north of the port of Duluth. Its production would surpass that of the Marquette basin. This deposit of an unexpectedly high grade of ore—over sixty percent iron—ran along the surface instead of requiring an underground operation, which made it possible to reduce the cost of extraction from $2.75 to $.045 cents per ton. That iron mountain would prove to be a boon to the American steel industry. A railroad was immediately built, and shipping began in 1892.

In 1893 John D. Rockefeller arrived on the scene. He was a Cleveland businessman who had been involved in refining oil from the deposit in Titusville, Pennsylvania, since 1865. Rockefeller was able to stake a claim on the Mesabi Range iron deposit and took almost total control of it. In 1895 he agreed to lease its operation to Andrew Carnegie, the big Pittsburgh steel maker, and in 1901 he sold it outright to John Pierpont Morgan, founder of U.S. Steel. Today, Michigan continues to produce 25 percent of the country's iron ore.

The exportation of the ore required that it be transported via railroad from the mines to the ports on the Great Lakes, where it was loaded onto ships. The transfer from one mode of transportation to the other occurred through the use of storage facilities, which had containers that unloaded their contents directly into the ships via chutes. Each of these portside warehouses extended along the lakefront for more than twelve hundred feet; a dozen of these massive wood, steel, or concrete structures survive today. The first of them, made of wood, was built in Marquette in 1857; the last, of concrete, dates from 1944 and is located in Thunder Bay, Ontario. In Manitowoc, on the western shore of Lake Michigan, south of Green Bay, a maritime museum recounts the commercial history of the Great Lakes.

The mining resources buried deep in the country's interior were still a great distance from the center of the metallurgical industry, located in the eastern part of the nation, between Pennsylvania and Lake Erie. The Great Lakes became a continuous, navigable waterway thanks to the construction of the Sault Sainte Marie Canals, which made it possible to circumvent the falls that had formerly barred navigation. The port of Cleveland was the hub for rail and waterway traffic headed for Pittsburgh and western Pennsylvania. Therefore, it is not surprising that the Hulett unloader, named after the engineer who perfected it in 1898, was designed and built in that city. The enormous jaw of the machine had the capacity to pick up nineteen tons of ore at once, thus reducing the price of unloading iron ore from just over $.17 to $.055 per ton. Once the site of trade for Ohio's agricultural products and raw materials, Cleveland began to handle most of Lake Superior's iron ore production at the turn of the century. Several examples of Huletts operated until fairly recently in the ore basin of the Pennsylvania Railroad. Unfortunately, these dinosaurs were too expensive to maintain and were abandoned by

Conrail in late 1992; the so-called lake carrier ships, which carry their own mechanical conveyor systems, now do their own unloading. The preservation of four of these machines in situ is currently at the center of a battle between port authorities and preservationists.

THE WESTERN MINING STATES: SILVER AND COPPER

The opening of silver mines in the Rockies set off another great mining rush in the history of the United States, after that spurred by the discovery of the resources in the Lake Superior region. California was the first area to be targeted, around the Comstock Mining District (whose decline began before 1870), and especially around the Silver Creek Mining District on the eastern slope of the Sierra Nevada Range. The development of that district led to the birth of a string of cities and the formation of Alpine County in what was a very isolated region with a very harsh environment.

Other states were part of that rush. In Utah, near Park City, the Silver King Mining Company supplied the mine, discovered in 1892, with high-performance equipment. For a long time, that site was the richest in the state, and perhaps in the world. The other major movement, in the last two decades of the nineteenth century, was associated with the shift of the center of the country's copper production farther to the West, more precisely, to southwestern Montana, around Butte and Anaconda. Butte was the capital of the industrial empire built by the Anaconda Copper Mining Corporation, which, in the early twentieth century, made the region the foremost global producer of copper, zinc, and manganese. The city inspired the modernist painter Louis Lozowick, who depicted it as it appeared in about 1926–27. A symbol of that industrial glory, one of the tallest smokestacks in the world (nearly six hundred fifty feet high), still survives.

In the early twentieth century, the last deposit of high-grade copper ore in the western United States was discovered in Kennecott, Alaska. This was the largest mining operation carried out in that state, and one of the largest mines of this type exploited

Top: *Miners using special ladders to go down to the mines and come back up (c. 1890).*

Bottom: *A group of miners about to be lowered down to the mines in a car, (c. 1902).*

Above: *Shaft No. 2 at the Quincy Mining Company in Hancock, Michigan, forms a picturesque American mining landscape, with its wood structures and row of conveyors.*

Opposite: *The Nordberg machine (1920) at the Quincy site, equipped with a low-pressure cylinder.*

Left: *The Quincy Mining Company's locomotives at Portage Lake.*

Below: *Ore processing.*

Above: *These enormous Hulett machines were used to unload ore ships in Cleveland, Ohio. Installed on a massive concrete base, they were maneuvered on rails. The ore port of the Pennsylvania Railroad Company, built in 1911–12, was the largest unloading port on the Great Lakes.*

Right: *An ore ship with its automatic unloading equipment.*

Above: *The steel headframe of the Stewart Mine in Butte, Montana.*

Right: *The Kennecott Silver Mine in Alaska.*

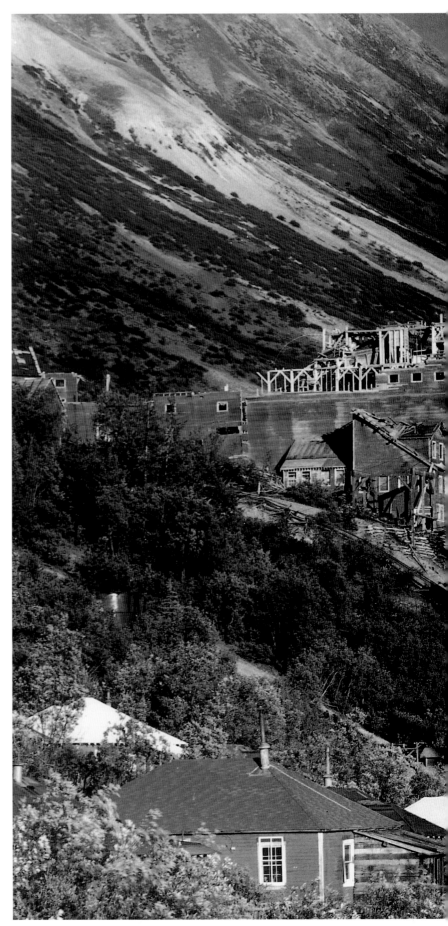

Right: *The Bingham Canyon Mine, exploited by the Kennecott Utah Copper Corporation, near Salt Lake City, Utah, was the largest open-pit mining site in the world.*

Below: *The quarry of the Hilltop Slate Company near Wells, Vermont.*

Right and below: *The entrance and access gallery to the saltpeter mine at Mammoth Cave in Kentucky.*

Above left: *A windmill for crushing sugar cane on the Whim plantation, St. Croix, the Virgin Islands.*

Above right: *An animal-driven mill on the same plantation.*

Left: *This steam engine with handle-operated cylinders crushed sugar cane (c. 1860) on the Adrian plantation in St. John, the Virgin Islands.*

Below left: *A modern coal facility in the Monongahela Valley, West Virginia.*

Below right: *Automatic coal-loading equipment on docked barges along the river.*

Above: *The Sault Sainte Marie hydroelectric plant in Michigan. The Saint Marys River and its rapids, first circumvented in 1855 by a canal for the needs of trade and navigation, were exploited for energy in 1898–1902, leading to the construction of what was at the time the largest hydroelectric plant in the world.*

Right: *The generator room at Sault Sainte Marie.*

in the country. The financing was supplied by the Alaska Syndicate, at the initiative of the Guggenheim family and of J. P. Morgan. Opened in 1911 and shut down in 1938, it had an unusually brief existence.

That mine, located west of Anchorage, in the Wrangell-St. Elias National Park and Reserve, near Kennecott Glacier, preserves particularly spectacular buildings. Their pyramid-shaped architecture of superimposed massive wood-frame structures, surprising as it may be, is not without counterparts in Europe. The forms are reminiscent of modern installations such as those of the Argentiera mines in Sardinia.

The central building housed ore storage facilities that were very technologically advanced. Outside the factory proper, forty-five additional buildings, an elevated light-rail system, and four mining camps compose an industrial landscape that has been classified as a national historic landmark, but which is nevertheless threatened by the deterioration that is inevitable in a very harsh climate.

THE INDUSTRIAL EXPLOITATION OF QUARRIES

There is little difference between an open-pit coal or copper operation and a quarry in the classic sense of the word, except in terms of the effect on the environment or the technology itself. Nevertheless, quarries extracting construction materials have attracted little attention among industrial archaeologists. Beginning in the nineteenth century, the increase in the number of quarries and the overexploitation of their resources have been linked to industrialization and its effects on the development of transportation and on urbanization.

Let us consider just two examples. The first has to do primarily with military history; there is a close relationship between the mobilization of resources and war efforts. Hence, saltpeter quarries played a key role in the manufacture of munitions during the Civil War. One of them, Mammoth Cave, in Edmonson County, Kentucky, has attracted the attention of the Historic American Engineering Record, both as a site of technological in-

terest and as a monument of national history. The quarry is now part of a national park, with the same status as the site of the Battle of Gettysburg, during which Union troops blocked the advance of Confederate soldiers in 1863.

The second example involves slate quarries located on the outskirts of the large urban zone extending from New York to Boston. At issue is colored slate, quarried since the late nineteenth century around Granville, New York, and Poultney, Vermont, and which in 1898 was the object of a report by the U.S. Geological Survey, based on maps established in 1894–96. These maps recorded some two hundred quarries concentrated in a zone about thirty-five miles long and four miles wide. At the height of their exploitation, in about 1900, sixty-four companies were operating in the area. Activity declined subsequently, and many quarries filled up with water; in the last few years, however, operations have resumed. The abandoned quarries created a landscape of artificial lakes, which was in marvelous harmony with the surrounding forested environment along the nearby Appalachian Trail. The presence of red, green, blue, or yellow tile on the roofs of homes in the Northeast is a reminder of that industrial episode.

Mines, quarries, and energy resources of all kinds are finding their legitimate place in the definition and preservation of the country's industrial heritage. Once judged inexhaustible, these enormous resources now appear threatened with destruction, like the architecture of the related industry. For specialists in the contemporary industrial heritage, there is no longer any difference between a mine in the West and a textile factory in New England. Both are part of the memory—the history—of the development of the country and of the people who have inhabited it. At this point, industrial archaeology verges on the archaeology of landscapes and ways of life.

ENERGY CHOICES

As we have already seen, in its first phase the history of energy production in the United States was very similar to that of

Western Europe, given the primacy granted to generous hydraulic resources, then the gradual shift to steam power. In the late nineteenth century, fossil fuels (coal and oil) were being used in massive amounts, the country being richly endowed in this domain by nature. Nevertheless, it was not long before the vital and strategic need to manage the use of these fuels and their reserves became apparent, and the country turned increasingly to importation. This caution was simultaneously extended to geological resources for farming, grazing, and forestry. In the second half of the twentieth century, the energy choices of the United States increasingly diverged from those of Europe, as demonstrated by the country's decision to privilege road transportation, to minimize the use of nuclear energy, and to even return to the use of renewable energy sources, such as wind (evidenced by the windmills that have sprouted up in California along the edge of the desert regions). At the same time, interest in the use of coal resources, which were far from exhausted, experienced a resurgence during the oil crisis and the Cold War, for reasons of economy and because of concerns about achieving energy independence.

The United States controls a small tropical region in the Caribbean. In 1917, among other possessions, it purchased from Denmark the archipelago of the Virgin Islands, located east of Puerto Rico. The Historic American Engineering Record became interested in studying the archaeological history that is apparent there, a very particular cycle of energy use. The small islands of St. Croix, St. Thomas, and St. John, lacking adequate hydraulic power, used animal power, windmills, and steam to harvest its main crop, sugar cane. The panorama is obviously very different there than in the sugar industry of Louisiana. In the mid-eighteenth century, only animal power was used in the islands; the yield of that technological system was low because of the exhausting effort required of the beasts (oxen or horses). In about 1750, the use of windmills to propel the crushers rapidly replaced the use of animals. Finally, steam became the preponderant energy source following the emancipation of the slaves in 1848; it allowed a much more rapid and efficient extraction of the

cane juice, and, as a result, revolutionized the entire process of sugar manufacture from its first phase.

STEAM POWER

The steam age began early in the United States, with the development of steam navigation on the Hudson and Mississippi Rivers in the early years of the nineteenth century, following the pioneering experiments of Robert Fulton and, a short time later, the first crossing of the Atlantic by a steamboat, the *Savannah,* in 1819.

In addition, the beginning of construction of the American railroad network was almost immediately accompanied by the introduction of an industry for building mobile steam engines—that is, locomotives. Baltimore was a pioneer in this respect, with Matthias Baldwin, a clockmaker originally from Philadelphia, launching that industrial sector in 1832. By the end of the Civil War, he had become the largest builder of steam locomotives in the country. In 1900, the Baldwin Locomotive Works produced more locomotives than all the other builders in the United States combined. It was also the foremost builder of locomotives in the world. The scale and volume of production at Baldwin induced the locomotive business to introduce innovations in the 1850s and 1860s, such as the standardization of certain equipment parts and even the division of labor, about twenty years before Frederick Taylor's ideas on scientific management made their appearance.

On an even larger scale, it was the requirements of iron and steel production, spurred by the demand for rails, that gave the major impetus to the search for coal and its extraction in the central Appalachian zone, and, in particular, for varieties used in the production of coke. The spread of steam power depended on the availability of coal resources.

THE INTRODUCTION OF OIL

Providence certainly did good work near the border of Pennsylvania and Ohio, in the richest part of the oil region that extends

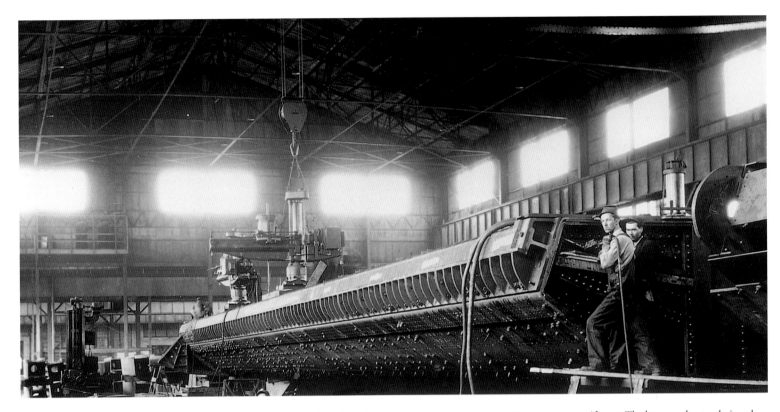

TWO WELDED DRAFT TUBE LINERS
13'1 1/2"DIAMETER TOP X 33'1" OVAL BOTTOM

BOULDER DAM PROJECT

BUILT BY BETHLEHEM STEEL COMPANY
LEETSDALE, PENNA.

Above: *The large steel gates designed for Bonneville Dam on the Columbia River in Oregon were manufactured in 1937 at the Bethlehem Steel Company factory in Pottstown, Pennsylvania. In the 1930s, that company provided components for many dams.*

Left: *The enormous welded steel pipes for Boulder Dam, on the Colorado River at the Arizona-Nevada border, were manufactured in 1936 at the Bethlehem Steel Company factory, located in Leetsdale, Pennsylvania.*

Opposite: *The irrigation dam in Little Rock, California, is a superb combination of concrete buttresses, braces, and arches.*

180

Above: *Electric substation No. 14 of the Interborough Rapid Transit Company, a line of the New York subway. Many of the old substations of the New York City Transit Authority survived into the 1990s. This one, at the corner of 96th Street and Broadway, fed the IRT line from 1904 to 1990.*

Above right: *The Concord gasholder in New Hampshire in 1888 and (top) the internal structure of the dome. Among a dozen survivors, all located in New England (with the exception of the one in Oberlin, Ohio), the Concord gasholder*

is notable as the only one that has not been converted to other uses, and whose internal equipment, including the mechanisms for raising and lowering the bell, has remained intact. The construction of a masonry casing around the pressurized metal tank of the gasholder protected it from inclement weather and allowed it to move properly up and down. The building shell also eliminated the pressure exerted laterally by the wind or by loads of snow on the roof, and prevented icing on the glides and pulleys, or in the shaft into which the gasholder was inserted. In addition, the brick walls protected against the risk of explosion.

from the southern part of New York state to Tennessee, where natural gas and oil are found in sedimentary formations of porous and permeable sandstone. It was in that zone, also recognized for its extraordinary wealth of coal, that, during the Civil War, the modern exploitation of oil came into being. This was not a true discovery: through the ages, oil had oozed from the soil there or had streamed from hillside rivers. It was used as an all-purpose medicine, as an excellent lubricant when mixed with flour, or as a fuel for lighting by the poor—in spite of its odor. In the Allegheny Valley north of Pittsburgh, oil came out mixed with salt water; it was called kerosene and also coal oil. In about 1840, the United States was looking for a source of lighting fuel that was better and less expensive than whale oil or candles, and less dangerous than the mixture of turpentine and alcohol. Hence, the interest that Atlantic Coast companies showed in the early 1850s in the oil of the Titusville region and the now-legendary Oil Creek Valley.

"Colonel" Edwin Drake, an agent from one of these companies, had the idea of looking for oil in the subsoil instead of being content with the surface discharge. With the help of rudimentary equipment manufactured locally, in 1859 he was the first to successfully drill for oil, reaching a layer of water and oil combined at a depth of about sixty-five to eighty feet. A local oil rush followed. After the Civil War ended, real speculation developed in the Buffalo-Cleveland-Pittsburgh triangle, giving birth to strange oil boomtowns, known as Red Hot, Pithole City, Tip Top, Babylon, and Petroleum Centre, and some of which had only a brief existence. In any case, the characteristic feature of the oil fields on the western slopes of the Appalachians was their fragmentation into a large number of deposits, a phenomenon linked to the diversity of the geological strata. The discovery of the Pithole deposit, along a small tributary of the Allegheny River in 1865, seemed to guarantee long-term production, which by then was dependent on the use of depth explosives to speed the flow of oil. Within three months, an urban area with a population of fifteen thousand was built up. The town ceased to exist in 1866 after several fires totally destroyed it. In the meantime, the

resources had dried up and the speculators had moved on to other drilling sites.

The oil was transported along the secondary waterways, either loaded directly or placed in barrels on flat-bottomed boats. On the Allegheny, steamboats and tugboats took over. Roads were also used to reach the Pennsylvania and Erie Railroad and, in 1865, the first train carrying oil began to run, with each car carrying two large cylindrical storage tanks. The main destinations were the refineries on the Atlantic Coast (Baltimore, Philadelphia, Camden, New York, and Boston) and Lake Erie; Cleveland took the lead in that industry.

John D. Rockefeller established a refinery in Cleveland in 1865. It was an excellent economic calculation, since the profitability of refining was much greater than that of production itself. There was thus a shift toward a system in which powerful commercial companies controlled a structure of production divided up among a great number of small businesses. Rockefeller opened a sales office in New York in 1867, and by 1869 his refinery was already classified as the largest in the world. Its owner was able to declare, "The oil business is mine." The company took the name Standard Oil of Ohio in 1870. In the following decade, exploration intensified in Pennsylvania; the search for particularly rich strata led the company to drill as deep as thirteen hundred feet.

Rockefeller stubbornly pursued a policy of buying up pipeline companies, controlling rail transport, and absorbing other refineries (twenty out of twenty-five in Pittsburgh, ten out of twelve in Philadelphia). In 1878, he had more than a ninety-seven percent monopoly on transport and greater than a ninety percent monopoly on oil refining in the United States. A permanent rivalry pitted the independent transporters and refiners, who were attempting to attack that monopoly, against Rockefeller, who regularly succeeded in buying them up. The federal government came to the aid of the independents with the Sherman Antitrust Act of 1890, but it was not until 1911 that a judgment forced Standard Oil of Ohio to split into thirty-four distinct companies.

In the early twentieth century, the nature of oil consumption changed completely, with a shift from lighting to locomotion. The gasoline engine needed only mass-produced fuel from deposits of inferior quality to run.

The geography of petroleum production, one century after its beginnings, has relegated Pennsylvania to fifth place among the oil-producing states, with only one percent of national production—behind Texas, California, Louisiana, and Illinois. But Pennsylvania still has large proven reserves and produces oil of superior quality, rich in paraffin, on which a lubricant industry of global importance is founded.

After 140 years of petroleum exploitation, temporary wood structures, light, metal-framed derricks, and the pipes supplying the shafts may not constitute a rich collection of archeological relics. Yet one of the technical components of the petroleum industry that left behind a great deal of evidence has recently begun to attract attention: the central energy distribution systems for pumping out crude oil. That technology, which began to develop in the 1880s, consisted of transmitting an alternating motion to about thirty shafts from a steam engine and, later, from an oil-driven engine, which needed no more than fifteen or twenty horsepower to operate. Another system worthy of attention consisted of injecting compressed air or steam into nearly exhausted deposits to reactivate the flow of the valuable product.

A NEW EPISODE IN WATER POWER

In the late nineteenth century, a new era began in the technology of harnessing water power. In the eastern half of the continent, hydroelectricity revived the method of exploiting the falls to produce energy, particularly those around the Great Lakes—Niagara Falls and the Saint Marys Falls. At the latter site, the beautiful thirteen-hundred-foot facade of the power station has been preserved; in the original plans, it was to have been the heart of a new industrial city, similar to Lowell, that never materialized because its remote location discouraged business activity. In about 1900, it was the largest hydroelectric plant in the world, producing forty thousand horsepower. From 1913 to 1963, it belonged to the Union Carbide chemical products company, which consumed all its energy.

To the west of the ninety-eighth western meridian (running down the middle of Kansas and Nebraska), which marks the beginning of the arid zone, average annual rainfall drops very rapidly. Most of the precipitation from the Pacific Ocean is intercepted by the Sierra Nevada and Cascade mountain ranges, where it usually falls at high altitudes in the form of snow. The runoff in May greatly adds to the indispensable water supply. Water had to be stored and redistributed via an irrigation system in order to facilitate Western settlement. That need led to the development of a particular technology for building very high dams to accommodate the steep waterfalls in the deep canyons. The dams had to achieve very high capacities and be exceptionally resistant to stress in order to bear the enormous pressure of water accumulated from the melting mountain snow.

The Tennessee Valley Authority initiative of the 1930s is well known; but, in fact, there had been federal programs to build dams in the West since the early years of the twentieth century. In 1902, the Reclamation Act had created the U.S. Reclamation Service, whose actions were implemented based on studies of the terrain previously conducted by the U.S. Geological Survey. The execution of these large public-works projects brought to light the difficulty of finding a technological solution that would make it possible to release water from very high dams, which were under tremendous pressure. It was just as tricky to release the water safely when it was needed as it was to build effective dam structures of earth, stone, or concrete in the first place. The research of Orville Hiram Ensign, an electrical engineer who had lived in southern California since 1893, brought about the implementation of the so-called needle-valve program. The first large project to use this design was the Roosevelt Dam (Arizona, 1903), followed by two other dams in Wyoming in 1906. The Little Rock Dam, in Los Angeles County, California, a structure designed for irrigation in 1922–24 by the engineer John S. Eastwood, was seven hundred fifty feet long and two hundred feet high; for fifty years it was the largest multiple-arch concrete dam in the world.

In 1925–30, thirteen dams were built, including the Mammoth Dam, so called because of its unprecedented size, and Boulder Dam (later renamed the Hoover Dam) on the Colorado River, on the border between Nevada and Arizona. Hoover Dam was designed both for hydroelectricity and for irrigation; whatever the dam's purpose, the construction technique was the same. Under study beginning in 1920, it was authorized by Congress in 1928. At a height of eight hundred feet, it constituted the largest work of civil engineering ever undertaken in the United States. The need for steel gates, valves, and pipes for these monumental projects earned various factories of the Bethlehem Steel Company a valuable customer base, especially when the market was stimulated by dam construction in the 1930s, the era of the New Deal.

CHAPTER 5

The Architecture of Industry

The heritage of industrial buildings in America provides an extremely rich repertoire of architectural forms. That richness lies, first and foremost, in the materials employed: wood, stone, brick, metal in various forms (iron, cast metal, steel), concrete, and glass. From the earliest date onward, these materials were often combined in innovative ways and always with an eye toward function. Various construction solutions, adapted to a broad range of industrial building types, coexisted in a single period. A typological analysis also contributes to an understanding of the richness of that heritage. A type of industrial building as particular as the grain elevator, for example, provides a true outdoor catalog of the successive use of different materials for the same purpose. Hence, in the Midwest, a collection of surviving grain elevators encapsulates the development of a building type over less than a century to serve the needs of an operation that first used wood, then steel, and finally concrete to preserve the bounty of the harvest.

The dialogue between clients, architects, and engineers involved in industrial architecture in the United States fostered research and experimentation—already seen in the case of bridges—as well as the evolution of models. The resulting architecture can be characterized by several factors: stylistic eclecticism, an attention to construction procedures that are best adapted to building safety, and a rigorous functionalism in the design of the factory. Albert Kahn was perhaps the modern paragon of American architects working on industrial buildings. Innovative in his construction methods and in the practice of his profession, Kahn has dominated the history of modern architecture for industrial use. Finally, it is important to consider that the industrial buildings of the United States, while providing a rich historical and architectural legacy, were designed with the priorities of production and commerce in mind. For this reason, a certain repetitiveness and uniformity in the architecture was to be expected and even de-

sired. The reproduction of architectural prototypes developed by specialized construction firms facilitated production and ensured an economy of scale while generally preserving a carefully executed style.

THE GENEALOGY OF TRADITIONAL FACTORIES

In New England and in Western Europe, industrial architecture began with the mechanical cotton- and wool-spinning mills. The first of these were very modest buildings, generally long and narrow (the power looms needed light from both sides), resembling country barns or flour mills, and stood little more than three stories high. Slater Mill measures about forty-three by thirty-three feet. The original buildings in Lowell were similar in configuration but larger in scale (about two hundred by fifty feet); however, none of the original four-story buildings survive intact today because of later reconstructions.

The materials used in the first phase of construction were wood for the framing and brick or stone masonry for the external walls. Later, cast-iron columns began to be used on the interior. Parallel rows of these columns supported the heavy floor loads that accommodated looms and workers, and which had to sustain tremendous levels of vibration. The design of the first textile factories exerted a predominant influence on nineteenth-century industrial architecture as a whole. In fact, its very simple, basic forms were adaptable to all sorts of industries and easily lent themselves to later expansion, either through additions to the ground floor or added stories. The use of wood and iron in combination persisted until the late nineteenth century—for example, at the Stearns factory in Cleveland, which manufactured automobiles—attesting to the respect architects had for these materials and this basic system of construction.

Entrepreneurs, builders, and especially insurance companies were particularly concerned with the risk of fire. The raw materials processed in the textile mills contained oily substances and the machines heated up in spite of lubricants. Even though the dangers were not on a par with those faced in the traditional grist mills (the mixture of air and flour could burst into flames

The waiting hall at Pennsylvania Station in New York, a few years before its demolition. The building was a remarkable example of early-twentieth-century architecture. Innovative metal structures of the era demonstrated their capacity to imitate architectural forms previously reserved for stone or brick.

spontaneously), engineers and specialists began to experiment early on with methods that made it possible to, if not eliminate the risks, then at least limit the damage by slowing the progression of fire. In 1827, the Manufacturers' Mutual Fire Insurance Company, founded by Zachariah Allen, a cotton worker from Rhode Island, recommended erecting brick walls in the form of piers and buttresses separated by large windows; doubling the thickness of the beams so that their excessive size would cause them to smolder rather than burn; specifying floors at least three inches thick, resting on mortar, in order to prevent the oil from the machines and the water from the pumps from moving from one floor to another; and using round support columns nine inches in diameter on the ground floor, preferably of pine or very dry oak. Floors were also already being built with iron framing and brick vaults covered with cement, and even with cast-iron support columns. All these formulas were modeled on the textile factories of England and had been recommended by William Strutt and Charles Bage in the 1790s. They were described in 1826 in *American Mechanics Magazine*.

A BRILLIANT INTERLUDE: CAST IRON IN NINETEENTH-CENTURY ARCHITECTURE

Cast-iron columns, though often used in the same capacity as wood, were criticized for their tendency to buckle when subjected to heat, or to break when they came into contact with the cold water used by firefighters, thus allowing the building to collapse. In 1860–80, however, cast iron, in the form of prefabricated components, enjoyed extraordinary favor for the facades of buildings to be used as workshops or warehouses in all the large industrial cities. In 1865, cast-iron fabricator Daniel Badger, a rival of James Bogardus (see below), published a deluxe catalog called "Architectural Ironworks of the City of New York." In 1973, the New York neighborhood known as SoHo (south of Houston Street in Manhattan) was classified as a national historic district.

In the 1840s, the architect and engineer James Bogardus (1800–1866), the son of a farmer in the Catskill region, became the advocate of the cast-iron construction process in the United States. At the age of seven, he had witnessed Robert Fulton going up the Hudson River to Albany in his steamboat, the *Clermont*, at the rate of five miles per hour. In the 1810s, he benefited from the scientific lectures delivered by Amos Eaton, the future founder of the Rensselaer Institute in Troy. In 1820, Bogardus left for Savannah, the port where, the previous year, the paddle-wheel steamer *Savannah* had been launched across the Atlantic to make its way to Saint Petersburg. In Savannah, Bogardus made the acquaintance of a young English architect, William Jay, who manufactured decorative cast-iron pieces for the homes of the local merchant class. From 1829 to 1836, Bogardus lived in New York, where the American Institute had just opened; like the Franklin Institute in Philadelphia, it was to become a central meeting place for metallurgists, mechanical engineers, and other inventors passionate about technological innovations. Bogardus was an inventor with a fertile mind, as his many registered patents show.

From 1836 to 1840, Bogardus stayed in England, a country where cast iron was already being produced in quantity and at a price that made it competitive as a building material. St. Katherine Dock in London, inaugurated in 1828 and built by the engineer Thomas Telford, had already attracted notice for its colonnade of massive cast-iron Doric columns, which supported a brick warehouse six stories high. This was only one example among many others, since cast iron was also used in the construction of aqueducts, bridges, aristocratic homes, and so on.

During a trip to Italy, Bogardus imagined building entire facades of cast iron, which would borrow the architectural style of classical antiquity and the Renaissance. Until that time, cast iron was used only for internal framing. However, Bogardus realized that it would allow for outer walls that would be lighter than the thick stone walls, thus requiring smaller foundations, and that these facades could be erected much more quickly thanks to the simple process of assembling hundreds (and sometimes thousands) of pieces of molded cast iron. The malleability of cast iron also made it possible to mass-produce ornamental motifs at a price much lower than that of sculpted stone. Finally, using cast iron offered a gain of both space and light. Bogardus returned to the United States determined to explore this new avenue.

Bogardus, who established himself in Manhattan as an independent businessman in 1842, was perfectly aware of the obsession of the time: the spread of fire in the urban environment. (New York had been ravaged by fire in 1835, and would be so again in 1845.) Convinced of cast iron's resistance to fire, and in opposition to public opinion that attributed all sorts of defects to the metal, he proclaimed himself "the builder of iron houses" and began to produce four basic components (apart from the ornamental pieces), which could be combined in different ways to vary the appearance of the building. In so doing, he was applying two modern principles: the technique of mass production and the interchangeability of parts. Publicity for his processes, which were patented in 1850, was guaranteed by the construction of his own factory in 1849, a four-story structure made entirely of cast iron. It was not long before Bogardus received a large number of orders. Outside New York, the large cities embraced the new cast-iron architecture: Philadelphia, Boston, Baltimore, San Francisco, Albany, Chicago, and many others as well. The vogue for this type of construction in Philadelphia was behind the growth of the Phoenix Iron Company, which later in the century became a powerful metal-construction firm. In 1856, Bogardus, now boasting the title "architect in iron," published a treatise on cast-iron construction and the advantages of buildings with iron facades.

Cast-iron architecture was used less for factories proper than for vertical towers, warehouses, and, above all, buildings for commercial use, multipurpose buildings that lent themselves to use by light industries of all kinds. The historical episode of the architecture of cast-iron facades is a good illustration of the ambiguity surrounding the use of the term *industrial architecture:* cast iron, certainly a quintessential industrial material, was in this particular case used for commercial-use buildings or offices, much more than for proper industrial use. The passion for rehabilitating these cast-iron-fronted buildings for the benefit of retail use, fashionable housing, offices, and entertainment centers has played a role in rescuing one aspect of the urban industrial heritage.

The era of cast-iron architecture, both in terms of framing and of facades (which, in fact, never precluded the use of brick for the construction of a building's other walls), was relatively brief, partly because the advantage of the process was rendered obsolete by the drop in the price of steel. In the 1880s, steel became the most commonly used, and the most supple, material for manufacturing metal frameworks for industrial buildings.

A TECHNICAL, FUNCTIONAL, AND STANDARDIZED ARCHITECTURE

The fire-prevention regulations of the 1830s were still being reprinted in manuals in the 1880s, despite the invention of the automatic fire sprinkler in 1879. The notion of slow-burning construction materials retained all its importance in industrial buildings, which were sometimes very large. The Factory Mutual Insurance Company and the Boston Manufacturers' Mutual Fire Insurance Company employed engineers to define a type of construction that would make it possible to control and even extinguish fires, and they reduced premiums for the industrialists who followed their recommendations. In 1905, the Factory Insurance Association published a collection of recommended building plans. Therein lies one of the sources of the eclipse of the architect in favor of the engineer: all ornament was now eliminated as constituting a pointless risk; the use of paint and other wall coverings was limited to a minimum, as was the presence of internal partitions that could interfere with the spraying of water. Attics (where fire is difficult to fight) were abandoned in favor of flat roofs. The central staircase was eliminated, and windows were enlarged as much as possible—signaling the beginning of the daylight factory. At that time people were still in shock from the huge fires that had ravaged Boston in 1872 and, especially, Chicago in 1871. Therefore, it was no accident that, from the 1870s to the 1910s, Chicago became the birthplace of an architecture of warehouses of a particularly well-researched design.

The engineers also recommended that the number of stories be reduced, with preference given to factories on a single level. In the early twentieth century, these factories, because they consumed much more space, encouraged industry to move to the outskirts of the city. The great Boston engineer Charles T. Main

The wood-frame grain elevator of the Farmers' Elevator Company in Herman, Minnesota.

Above: *The concrete grain elevator of the Herman Market Company in Herman, Minnesota.*

Left: *The Pioneer Steel Elevator in Minneapolis, Minnesota.*

Above: *The central yard of Boott Mills, between factories 2 and 6, in Lowell, Massachusetts.*

Opposite, top left: *The shops of the F. B. Stearns Company in Cleveland, Ohio. The interior of this former automobile factory, dating from the late nineteenth century is remarkable for the persistence of its use of older building technology. The construction system combines a strong wood frame with steel saddles.*

Opposite, top right: *A nineteenth-century wood staircase at Mount Vernon Mills No. 2 in Baltimore, Maryland, once an open invitation to fire.*

Opposite, bottom: *The articulation of wood and cast-iron supporting members in an old woolen mill in Harrisville, New Hampshire.*

Above and opposite: *Cast-iron facades in downtown Manhattan.*

Left: *The daylight factories in Lowell, Massachusetts, along the Merrimack River. Improved lighting and safety were key features in the evolution of the factory. In the early twentieth century, so-called skeleton construction in concrete or steel allowed for more fenestration than was possible with load-bearing walls.*

Below: *A playing-card factory in Brooklyn, New York, near the Manhattan Bridge.*

Opposite: *The demolition of the original site of the Colgate Palmolive Company in Jersey City, New Jersey, began in 1988, after 120 years of cumulative development. This building housed production lines for bar soap and laundry detergent. It was topped by a luminous clock visible from Manhattan, which was saved and reinstalled on the site. The architectural elegance of the building is achieved through its articulated concrete skeleton, its generous fenestration spaced in a regular pattern, and the stringcourses and cornices that break the monotony of the facade.*

Left: *A clothing factory from the early twentieth century in Baltimore.*

Below: *A twentieth-century Baltimore warehouse with austere concrete facades.*

Above: *A machine shop in Bethlehem, Pennsylvania.*

Right: *The Rogers locomotive shop in Paterson, New Jersey.*

Right: *The Assembly Building of the Chrysler-Dodge factory, in Warren, Michigan, is remarkable both for its vast open interiors, which would later be of great interest to builders of airplanes, and for its metal frame designed to support a glass roof, with its unexpected but carefully calculated slopes.*

Overleaf: *The Export Building of the Chrysler-Dodge Half-Ton Truck Plant in Warren, Michigan (1938). Designed by Albert Kahn, this factory is the best-known example of his industrial buildings. Its planar facade and sharply defined shapes, transparency, and the originality of its roof structure create a striking architectural presence. In ensuring the triumph of natural light and open work spaces, Kahn profoundly revolutionized industrial architecture and contributed significantly to the economic success of the American automobile industry.*

130890

The American Brewery in Baltimore, Maryland, built in 1887 for the brewer John Frederick Weissner, is one of the most remarkable examples of the "Teutonic Brewery" style still surviving in the United States.

praised these new low factories, in which the problem of vibrations practically disappeared. In the multistory factories, however, masonry walls gave way to framing made of concrete (Ernest Rasom experimented with that material beginning in the 1880s) and steel. Such structures were economical to assemble and resistant to heavy loads and fire. In that evolution as a whole, one can grasp the shift that led to the architectural engineering of Albert Kahn. In fact, studying Kahn offers an opportunity to examine the shift in the balance between the two professions—architecture and engineering. In the United States, an architect's training and profession were largely unorganized, while engineers could apprentice as architects if need be. In the twentieth century, engineering organizations became the birthplace of serious interest in the industrial heritage.

In 1900–20, thousands of uniform concrete-frame factories proliferated, without applied decoration but of high quality. This factory model was technically perfect when compared to all the rest of civil architecture. The popular model was a five-story building with large windows, brick infill in the exterior walls, and, on the interior, beams and thick columns made of gray concrete. These thousands of projects, which shaped the industrial landscape from one end of the country to the other during this period, came from large architecture and engineering firms, of which Albert Kahn's firm was a pioneering example. The preeminent firms that were active at that time were Giffles & Vallet, Smith, Hinchman & Grylls, and Lockwood & Greene.

This stripped-down architecture responded to the desire of industrialists to have inexpensive, flexible workspaces, but also to the spread of a new aesthetic, one that represented a culture of modernity, efficiency, applied science, and trust in new materials. Hence, the seemingly generic architecture of industrial buildings in the twentieth century created objects of cultural significance that resulted from the changes that had come about in trade, architecture, and technology.

Another tradition of industrial architecture went through a parallel evolution: the development of vast open workspaces, which continued to adapt to the growing requirements of the iron and steel industry, arsenals, and shipyards. The most classic type of arsenal was the large brick building with large semicircular arched openings. The Watervliet arsenal provides a superb late example. The shop where cannons designed for coastal fortifications were manufactured, built beginning in 1889, is the model of a workspace adapted to the requirements of moving large equipment parts and of providing adequate natural light.

Later, the automobile, aeronautic, and naval factories capitalized on the most radical possibilities of metal- and concrete-frame structures, thus freeing up the workspace to the maximum. It was in this field that Albert Kahn's iconoclastic principles prevailed. They had been formulated in the 1920s, by Kahn and his younger brother, Moritz, in complete contradiction of the traditional habits of stylistic and ornamental decoration on industrial buildings. Like the industrialist, the architect who built for industry was guided, in the first place, by the concern to eliminate needless expense. As Kahn saw it, the design of the industrial building had to be rigorously suited to the needs of the entrepreneur, which were determined by the organization of the production process: this meant eliminating any obstacle to the regular work flow, from the arrival of the raw materials to the delivery of the finished product. Along the way, nothing was to disturb the circulation of the products being assembled: the number of interior support columns had to be limited to a minimum, both to respond to that imperative and to reduce the construction cost. These concerns were combined with that of improving the working conditions by promoting circulation of air and light. Consideration for the exterior appearance of the industrial building was not eliminated, however, since Kahn thought that it was important for the image of the business, as well as for the positive influence it could exert on the workers themselves. But it was understood that a new aesthetic was to come about spontaneously from the quality of the design and materials, and from the interplay of lines and geometric volumes. The new factory, a perfect production machine, was to produce its own beauty through the expression of its functionality.

One of the best illustrations of these concepts is without a doubt Chrysler's Half-Ton Truck Plant, in Warren, in the Detroit area, which was built in 1937 to produce light trucks. In a very

Right: *The facade of the Lehigh Coal and Canal Building in Jim Thorpe, Pennsylvania, features a wealth of terra-cotta ornament.*

Below left: *The Bromo-Seltzer tower near the old port in Baltimore, a copy of the tower of the Palazzo Vecchio in Florence, is a picturesque monument to the popularity of Italian Renaissance architectural models among early-twentieth-century American architects and their clients.*

Below right: *The train station in Woonsocket, Rhode Island, is more suggestive of a station in a seaside resort than one in a capital of the wool industry.*

Opposite: *The train station in Point of Rocks, Maryland, on the B&O Railroad line is one of several stations on this line that adopted a High Victorian Gothic style.*

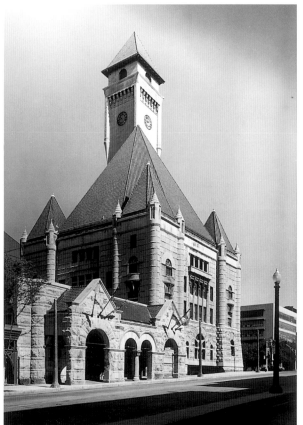

Above, left and right: *Union Station in St. Louis, Missouri.*

Right: *Union Station in Los Angeles displays the Mission Revival style popular in the region.*

Opposite: *The waiting room in Union Station in St. Louis. This almost Byzantine taste for luxurious decoration on the walls and ceilings is also found in what has become a chic restaurant in the old Pittsburgh train station (Station Square), and in the grand gallery of the Fisher Building in Detroit, designed by Albert Kahn, who was capable of indulging in eclecticism when he chose, and in response to his clients' tastes.*

Top left: *The Detroit train station, dating from 1913, is reminiscent of the Beaux-Arts style of Grand Central Station in New York, built by the same architectural firms, Warren & Wetmore and Reed & Stern.*

Left: *Camden Station in Baltimore. The first train station, built in 1856, was burned down during a major strike in 1877, which affected the entire B&O line.*

Top right: *A concrete structure with brick trim, this 1920s building is typical of civil architecture of the era, with large windows and ornamentation concentrated at the two upper stories.*

Above: *The original Westinghouse factory in Wilmerding, Pennsylvania. George Westinghouse (1846–1914) registered 360 patents between 1865 and 1918.*

Right: *Buildings at the Charlestown Navy Yards in Boston feature handsome decoration—brickwork in relief and a combination of granite and brick details.*

Below: *One of the shops at the Watervliet arsenal in New York State was designed in the style of Italian Renaissance churches.*

Bottom left: *This large shop in Boston's Charlestown Navy Yards has been converted to residential use.*

Bottom right: *The Fisher Building in downtown Detroit.*

Top: *A thermoelectric power station south of Chicago.*

Above: *The interior of the Port Richmond thermoelectric power station northeast of Philadelphia.*

Right: *The Colgate plant in Jersey City, New Jersey, with its exposed metal machinery and open-air catwalks, is a departure from traditional factory architecture.*

212

pure, formal composition, one of the two buildings combines a steel framework with vast glass surfaces, mounted on the foundation of a low brick wall, while a metal framework with a complex design supports plate-glass skylights with a carefully calculated slope. Beginning in 1940, the war effort again stimulated improvements in the design and rationalization of the work process, as attested to by the extraordinary success of the Chrysler Tank Arsenal in Detroit. The roofs definitively abandoned the formulas used for sheds in order to allow for flexibility in the assembly lines. Albert Kahn used horizontal windows at varying angles, hence the unusual shape of the roofs. The roof-wall combination produced extraordinary fenestration with a great sense of transparency, whose beauty struck the Bauhaus architects and Le Corbusier, who was already a champion of the cylindrical concrete grain elevators. But this tremendous achievement signaled a break between the engineers and industrialists on the one hand, and the architects on the other: American architecture magazines did not publish pictures of Albert Kahn's factories.

TURN-OF-THE-CENTURY ECLECTICISM

The increasingly technical and functional character of industrial buildings did not necessarily obliterate architectural ornament and stylistic references, which were borrowed from the architecture of the past and applied to the facades, sometimes for symbolic reasons. One of the most astounding examples is the architecture of breweries, which often displays its German heritage in its design. Many large cities, including Milwaukee, Pittsburgh, and Baltimore, had several dozen breweries in the early twentieth century, operated primarily by German immigrants. Only a few examples of the Teutonic-style brewery, made fashionable particularly by the architect Charles Stoll of Brooklyn, survive today. In Baltimore, the American Brewery was built for the brewer Frederick Weissner in 1887, a time when the city and its surrounding area had no fewer than twenty-one breweries. Residents called it the Germanic Pagoda. In Denver, Colorado, during the same years, the Tivoli Union Brewery, first called the Milwaukee Brewery, bore a name evoking the Tivoli Gardens in Copen-

hagen, which, like Munich, was a major European beer producer. It shut down all operations in 1969 but escaped destruction. Its prominent tower, in the Italianate style, stands watch over a business and convention center in downtown Denver.

Architectural eclecticism also enjoyed free rein in the construction of train stations in the late nineteenth century. Several of those on the B&O line adopted a "Swiss chalet" style: for example, in Point of Rocks, Maryland; Woonsocket, Rhode Island; and Jim Thorpe, in the Lehigh Valley of Pennsylvania, where, on opposite sides of a small square, the station faces the Coal and Canal Building, a superb interpretation of an Italian Renaissance palazzo. Other notable stations employed the Spanish style, such as Union Station in Los Angeles, or a composite style combining the Romanesque Revival on the exterior with motifs inspired by the Renaissance on the interior, as, for instance, Union Station in Saint Louis, Missouri.

Architectural ornamentation of factory buildings appealed to the most important entrepreneurs of the late nineteenth century and early twentieth century. Evidence of this can be found in the stylistic evolution of the Westinghouse complex in Wilmerding, Pennsylvania, which, from the 1880s to the 1920s, erected Germanic-style buildings, shops with elegant brick facades adorned with geometric motifs in relief, and small skyscrapers with the upper levels adorned with cornices and monograms. Unfortunately, it seems that efforts to save on maintenance costs have resulted in concealing these attractive buildings behind inappropriate metal siding. Government industries, as in the arsenals and shipyards of Boston and Watervliet, New York, also commissioned buildings with astonishing architectural touches, combining granite and brick in ornamental motifs worthy of palace architecture or concealing the manufacture of armaments behind Baroque facades.

Albert Kahn, who is best known for his functional, industrial designs, produced a great deal of eclectic architecture. In numerous private and public commissions, he demonstrated his capacity to draw from an almost encyclopedic repertoire of architectural history. After twenty years practicing his profession, in the 1920s he was commissioned to undertake a grandiose project sponsored by the major automobile industrialists in Detroit: to build a new business district close to their factories, away from the historic city center located on the Detroit River, in order to relieve the congestion in that area.

The project began in 1922 with the General Motors Building (the General Motors Company had just come into being through the merger of Buick, Cadillac, Oldsmobile, and Chevrolet). Kahn chose an austere plan for its administrative headquarters, four rectangular blocks reaching 210 feet in height, and including fourteen stories of offices. On the two lowest stories, however, the facades were adorned with arcades and colonnades inspired by Greek architecture. Nearby, and again in a style removed from the functionalism reserved for the factories, Kahn then built the Fisher Building in 1928–29 for the six Fisher brothers. They had accumulated a colossal fortune manufacturing automobile and airplane bodies, and they refused to impose a fixed budget on Kahn for the realization of their architectural showpiece. Dominated by a twenty-eight-story central tower (440 feet tall) situated at an angle, with a dining room at the top where the brothers and their mother regularly met, the L-shaped building combines a reinterpreted Gothic style with the abstract vertical style of the Finnish architect Eliel Saarinen, whose recent compositions in the United States had clearly fascinated Kahn. Kahn's work received the silver medal from an architectural society, which designated it the most beautiful commercial-use building of the year. In any case, the Fisher Building is a key landmark in the Detroit skyline. It has been called "the largest objet d'art" in the city, which may be an allusion to its central gallery, with its painted vaults, copper light fixtures and elevator doors, and abundant gilding and marble of all kinds, imported from around the world.

Today, the central district of Detroit is a fragile reminder of the city's industrial history, as attested to by its isolation in the middle of a devastated zone. Yet it remains a destination for lovers of twentieth-century American architecture. In the heart of the area the headquarters of Albert Kahn Associates, built by its founder in the 1930s, still stands.

FACTORY ARCHITECTURE: BETWEEN DEATH AND REBIRTH

It sometimes happens that businesses repudiate their own architectural legacy because of the high cost of maintaining it. It also sometimes happens that, after demolishing their real estate assets, the only remnants of their corporate image are advertising props that would be better suited to an industrial Disneyland, such as the giant Uniroyal tire on the edge of a highway in Detroit. Many heavy industries have moved away from the notion of using architecture to establish a corporate image and are moving toward a packaged-architecture design, which can be split into modules or modified at will; or their architecture takes the form of housing for hi-tech machinery.

Nevertheless, the functionality of forms and materials that has invigorated American industrial architecture for 150 years still produces aesthetically pleasing buildings. Brick lends itself to sturdy, modular architecture and remains a trimming of choice for structures requiring other materials. As for the vast hangars and factory floors, whose dimensions are determined solely by technical requirements, they continue to inspire certain awe—large electric power stations, which by tradition incorporate restrained ornamentation in their rigorous industrial architecture, are a case in point.

PART 3

Understanding Our Industrial Heritage

CHAPTER 6

Industrial Landscapes, Industrial Wastelands

In the United States, as in Europe, land clearing, rural settlement, and crop and stock farming were the major factors that shaped the landscape. Despite this human intervention, the resulting landscape took on the character of a natural setting. In reality, it came about from the pushing back of the vast primal forest in favor of what was, in fact, an artificial setting, developed according to different technical, legal, and social methods of exploiting agricultural resources and to different modes of assembling and dispersing settlements of people.

In comparison, the landscapes resulting from the development of industrial activities are much more recent and localized. Although for decades these activities were inserted into woodlands or bucolic landscapes without much intrusion, the rift they created in the environmental fabric appeared to contemporaries as an assault. With hindsight, these developments are perceived as both hostile and fascinating. Industry has ceased to extend its grasp, unlike urbanization, which now appears to be a poorly controlled tendency that was much more destructive in the end than industry was to the "countryside," rightly or wrongly identified with "nature." The traces of industrialization sometimes disappear swiftly, without proper research and documentation, thus threatening the important heritage of the industrial landscape that developed over the last two centuries.

INDUSTRY ALONG THE WATER

Into the late nineteenth century, the loyalty of many industries to hydraulic energy and the use of local cut stone as a building material for factories contributed toward maintaining a remarkable

The base of a smokestack dating from 1855 in Savannah, Georgia. The lower part of the 130-foot-tall smokestack is encased in a tank, made of decorated cast iron, which has a capacity of four hundred thousand gallons of water. It belonged to the shops of the Georgia Railway Company and served to evacuate vapors from the forge and the boiler.

harmony between even large plants and the surrounding environment, which was still relatively pristine. In certain Connecticut river valleys, the textile industry created sites that were aesthetically pleasing and harmonious with the landscape, such as Willimantic, where a large linen-weaving mill was created in 1854; it was converted into a thread factory when use of the sewing machine began to be widespread.

The old iron and steel industry also melded well with the landscape that had emerged when the land was first settled. One example is the Mount Etna Ironworks, near Juniata, Pennsylvania, a foundry and blast furnace that dates from 1807; it was active until 1877. Up to the Civil War, it was the primary producer of charcoal-fueled cast iron in the United States. Around the old-style furnace, which is modest in height, the components of a perfectly hierarchized housing settlement, combining beautiful granite and wood-frame construction, have been preserved and restored.

There are aspects of the industrial legacy that are not considered to be completely unsympathetic to the natural environment. For many generations, stone road or railroad bridges and viaducts have been appreciated as elements of the built environment that enhance, rather than disrupt, the visual balance of their landscapes or topography. Mining, though generally predatory, and noteworthy for causing an accumulation of debris that disturbs the environmental balance, sometimes exists in relative harmony with the surrounding forest and with the nearby waterways that facilitate the rapid distribution of coal to places far from the production sites. Such is the case for the coalfields of West Virginia that spread up and down the Monongahela Valley. Canals, an important accompaniment to industrialization, have a tendency to blend into their natural settings once they become inactive.

These relatively minor intrusions gave way to more damaging and exploitative development some decades later, as businesses grew larger and industry exerted a stronger presence in the environment. At that time, businesses took over vast areas of available land in seemingly arbitrary locations. Thus, for example, a copper ore processing plant stands in a setting of virgin mountains in Alaska; and the furnaces of the cement works in Coplay, Pennsylvania, invade the site of an old rural settlement in the Lehigh Valley. Yet the intrusion became the landscape in turn, and was accepted as such by the surrounding population, for which the industry provided employment.

CREATING THE URBAN ENVIRONMENT

Early in the country's history, industry, either by creating population centers or by inserting itself into preexisting urban centers, was responsible for developing individualized factory districts, with or without workers' housing. That individualization was premised on the technological support of a system for distributing hydraulic energy via the diversion of canals.

Lowell, Massachusetts, and Paterson, New Jersey, still provide fine evidence of this type of planning, thanks to the survival of a certain density of buildings and to their stylistic homogeneity. The brick architecture, which often features brick ornamentation, is characterized by monumental multistory elevations that borrow elements from Renaissance or Neoclassical models, which are skillfully superimposed onto the otherwise utilitarian buildings. The partial survival, and, more recently, the rehabilitation of these urban blocks can be attributed to a phenomenon known as preservation by neglect. In these mid-sized cities, as opposed to larger metropolises, there was less pressure to redevelop the areas occupied by the factories, even though they had been closed for a relatively long time.

COMPANY TOWNS

In the second half of the nineteenth century, large American companies spawned urban communities around them known as company towns, the workers' housing complexes that were built on the initiative of management. Many examples survive. The golden age of such paternalistic practices lasted until the eve of World War II. The company town represented a major contribution to urbanization in the United States. Today, these properties survive in the hands of other tenants or owners; usually they are well integrated into the surrounding urban fabric, which generally shares the same dominant housing model. Often, the building stock of the company town is of the same, if not a higher, quality than more recent urban developments.

In the mid-nineteenth century, Baltimore's textile manufacturers had tried to create an autonomous landscape linking workplaces to residences within the somewhat undeveloped valley of the Johns Falls River, now incorporated within the city. On either side of the river, neighborhoods of workers' houses faced the factory yard and tower, the two further connected by flights of stairs on the steep slopes that were designed for the workers' convenience. A similar layout was used at the end of the century in Wilmerding, Pennsylvania, where the Westinghouse workers, housed on the hillside, were provided with shortcuts passing under the train tracks, so that they could get to their workplace more easily. In the largest industrial cities—for example, in Pittsburgh and Johnstown—a modernized version of that practice took the form of cable cars serving the lower part of town.

The Lake Calumet area south of Chicago, which is now the terminal point in United States territory of the Saint Lawrence Seaway, became very industrialized after fire ravaged the city in 1871. The locale is noted, in particular, for metallurgical factories. Not far away, Pullman City survives intact, the most famous of American company towns. Paradoxically, it gained notoriety as the site of a hard-hitting workers' rebellion in the last years of the nineteenth century, a demonstration of the failure in the social-appeasement policy advocated by management. In hindsight, that policy may appear to have been grounded precisely in the success of thoughtful urban planning and the creation of a carefully maintained lifestyle, even if it no longer corresponds to current aspirations and standards of space and comfort. Assigned to the architect Solon S. Beman in 1881 by the owner, George Pullman, the company town had the goal of housing twelve thousand workers. It was organized into two complexes flanking the factory shops, which were arranged around the office building and its symbolic clock tower. That relationship is still perfectly intelligible, since most of the shops remain intact, though now occupied by other businesses.

Although the newest neighborhood, built in the twentieth century, is planned with an ordinary linear layout, the first town, in contrast, was organized around a true urban center. It included an esplanade, next to which stood the company hotel, built to lodge customers; a monumental freestone church; and a circular plaza with arcades and a covered market at its center. The architecture reveals an Italian Renaissance influence, the source of frequent borrowings among nineteenth-century architects. The principle adopted for the layout of the housing was not a grid, but long parallel paths bordered by trees. The houses, generally of two stories, are attached, with facades perfectly aligned on the street side, and with small service areas—not yards—extending in back. Although the foremen's houses are located along the edge of the central garden and have an additional story under the eaves and a more luxurious appearance, and although the buildings surrounding the market look just like middle-class homes, it cannot be said that the housing was strictly arranged into a hierarchy by location and comfort level. The complex as a whole, in fact, is characterized by the absence of any formal repetitiveness, with a juxtaposition of architectural forms and styles that alternate from one street to the next. Today, former Pullman workers have retained ownership of their houses and maintain them, as well as the grounds, with the same fastidiousness as residents in any other middle-class neighborhood. Over the long term, therefore, a remarkable sense of the defunct company's identity has survived, the memory of a world-renowned brand of rolling railroad stock. Also remarkable is the surviving sense of belonging to a community that has been broken up, but whose standard of living is still seen as exceptional, surrounded as it now is by an ordinary and impoverished urbanized area characteristic of the vast southern suburbs of Chicago.

In Trenton, New Jersey, the second generation of Roeblings, the largest manufacturers of steel cable in the United States, moved the company away from the Chambersburg district, where it was outgrowing its space. In 1904, Charles Roebling acquired 150 acres of land nine miles south of the city, in the town of Kinkora, along the Delaware River and close to a line of the Pennsylvania Railroad. He saw no other solution than to build, near his new factories, a town to house his employees and their families. In a phase of American history when ethnic diversification through immigration was changing large industrial cities like Trenton, the business could not hope to recruit its labor on site; the offer of housing was indispensable. For the Roeblings, the benefit of the operation was that it significantly delayed the unionization of their workers (until the early 1940s) and elicited remarkable loyalty from the labor force: in the mid-twentieth century, a number of employees had between thirty-five and fifty years of service.

The Roeblings, unlike George Pullman, were in no way idealists or social reformers driven by the desire to build a model city. Charles Roebling, however, built 750 homes of very fine quality—beautiful brick structures with slate roofs—hoping that the rent would constitute interest on the investment (1.5 million dollars by 1920). He added all sorts of conveniences and services: a post office, a hotel with a bar (the only one in town, thus easy to control), a general store, a grocery store, a bakery, a barber shop, a fire station, a hospital, a bank, a community hall with a library, a playing field, and even a prison. Quite simply, the Roeblings knew that an employer, if he wished to spur the loyalty and productivity of his employees, had to guarantee them something beyond the cost of their labor. These employees, by creating a school in 1908, expressed a desire to contribute to the Americanization of their children.

The houses had a minimum of four rooms on two levels, with gas lighting, coal-stove heating, running water, and toilets

Above: *Group housing for forge workers in Mount Etna, Pennsylvania, dating from the early nineteenth century.*

Right: *The Mount Etna blast furnace, with its bellows hole. In the twenty years following the American Revolution, one hundred fifty furnaces were put into operation in Pennsylvania, particularly in the central and eastern part of the state.*

Opposite, top: *The blacksmiths' houses, dating from the early 1830s.*

Opposite, bottom: *The boarding house for unmarried workers.*

Left: *The silk factory district of Paterson, New Jersey.*

Bottom left: *A view from the ground of the silk factory district, which has been partly demolished.*

Opposite, top: *An axonometric projection of the Rogers locomotive shops (c. 1906), drawn up by an insurance company. Beginning in 1829, the factory was served by one of the branches of Paterson's water diversion system. It first manufactured textile machines and paper machines, before taking part in the burgeoning locomotive market in the 1850s.*

Opposite, bottom: *One of the first of the Rogers factories.*

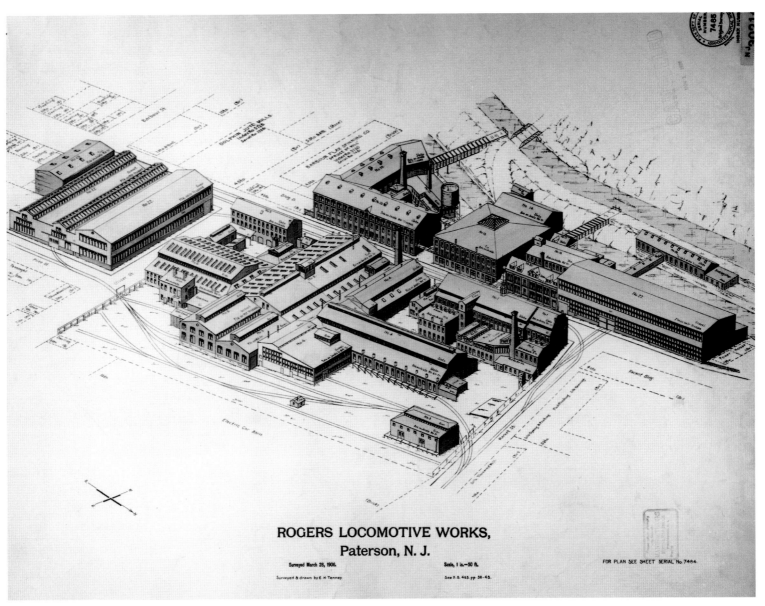

ROGERS LOCOMOTIVE WORKS,
Paterson, N. J.

Surveyed March 28, 1906.

Scale, 1 in.=50 ft.

Surveyed & drawn by E. H. Tenney.

See R.B. 445 pp. 38-45.

FOR PLAN SEE SHEET SERIAL No. 7484.

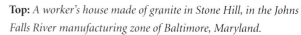

Top: *A worker's house made of granite in Stone Hill, in the Johns Falls River manufacturing zone of Baltimore, Maryland.*

Center: *The workers' houses of the Westinghouse Company in Wilmerding, Pennsylvania.*

Bottom: *The Pullman railway equipment factory in Pullman City, Illinois, designed to build luxury train cars, was built in 1880. The infamous 1894 strike, set off by a reduction in salaries, led to thirteen deaths before federal troops intervened. Closed in 1982, the factory was purchased by the state of Illinois, and a foundation is working to preserve it. Unfortunately, in December 1998 a fire destroyed the administration building and its clock tower.*

Pullman City: the marketplace (top), the foremen's houses (above left), the Florence Hotel (above right), and workers' houses (right).

linked to the sewer in an outbuilding on the premises. The skilled steelmakers were entitled to four to six rooms, generally with electric lights, a bathroom, and a laundry room in the basement. The foremen and department managers were assigned freestanding houses with a view of the park and the river, built in the Colonial style on two levels, with eleven rooms, including an entry hall; these homes had central steam heating. All the houses received free water, electricity, and sewer. Teams of maintenance staff replaced the paint and wallpaper free of charge every three years, and any maintenance problem was taken care of in a few hours. Was this the expression of an altruistic philosophy? Not at all: it simply expressed the conviction that a better quality of life than Trenton could offer would allow the company to hold on to its workers. In return, the waiting list for housing was a way to exert pressure, allowing the employer to reward loyal and faithful workers and to get rid of troublemakers. He could evict undesirable workers from company housing at any time; however, it does not appear that Roebling abused that power.

In Sparrows Point, Maryland, far from the center of Baltimore, the Bethlehem Steel factory created one of the most methodical and hierarchically organized housing developments of the late nineteenth and early twentieth centuries. The project began as an experiment and led to the birth of a company town with five thousand residents by 1940. It was designed for steelworkers and employees in the shipyards and their families. The organization of different types of row houses divided the residents into several strata. On A Street, on the edge of a peninsula that cut into Chesapeake Bay, was the home of the chief executive officer. B and C Streets held housing for upper management. D Street had businesses and services, as well as housing for the upper levels of the staff. Foremen and white skilled workers were lodged on E and F Streets. The houses here consisted of four rooms and looked out on a comfortable front porch. G Street functioned as a racial boundary: black workers were confined to H, I, J, and K Streets.

In the mid-nineteenth century, as a function of the new iron and steel industry, many large, unusually shaped factories, work spaces, and smokestacks that filled the sky with streams of smoke, were introduced into the landscape. The Cambria Iron Works, one of the first of its kind, lay behind the growth of the city of Johnstown, Pennsylvania. It is a jarring contrast to the surrounding countryside, an impression that was already rendered in pictures dating from the 1860s. Today, the old section of town is a faded environment of workers' neighborhoods, impoverished except for the churches, and archaic industrial buildings.

At the turn of the twentieth century, another generation of iron and steel factories arrived, whose size and layout were so immense that they overwhelmed the landscape around them. The change in scale is evident when one compares two views, composed from an almost identical angle but three-quarters of a century apart, which show Bethlehem, Pennsylvania, when it was still an idyllic rural setting, and what Bethlehem Steel Company made of it in the early years of the twentieth century.

During that period, the proliferation of factories of a single type, or of a group of businesses in close proximity linked by a subcontracting system, established industrial districts that were served by transportation and distribution networks. Several areas where this type of development occurred are easily identifiable. First, there is Pittsburgh and the very particular structure of its industrial core, which formed in the heart of the city and extended out via the waterways to both sides of the Monongahela, Allegheny, and Ohio Rivers. The fragility of this industrial landscape has become very clear, given that it has been radically eliminated from downtown Pittsburgh. A high-rise area and green space have taken its place, behind which the former industrial uses have become unintelligible. The many bridges offer a clue to the significance the steel age once had in that city.

In the areas surrounding the major east coast ports—from Baltimore on the banks of the Chesapeake Bay, to the Delaware River corridor between Philadelphia and Trenton, to New York Bay—industry's colonization left little room for other uses of the land and set up a barrier to the waterfront. Near the large metropolises—New York, Chicago, and, to a lesser extent, Buffalo—the most coherent and self-contained types of recent industrial landscapes are evident. While New York and Chicago developed as powerful urban entities, their growth and organization were never focused on narrowly industrial activities. Such activities were relegated to the outskirts, in jarring contrast to the city itself, as if some invisible wall separated the zones.

In the case of New York City, the Hudson River sets the city apart from its western outskirts, a large industrial zone in New Jersey, dedicated to the "dirty work" of the large metropolis. All sorts of industrial, storage, and transportation functions have been inserted into the usable patches of the Meadowlands, a marshy area that discourages urbanization. Historically, these functions were sustained by the role the zone played as the terminal point of eastbound traffic, before the obstacle of the river had been overcome with bridges and tunnels. In Chicago, the industrial city was established on the boundaries of the prestigious urban center, bounded on the west by the Chicago River and on the east by Lake Michigan. The terminals of different railway companies form clusters of railroad tracks, which extend toward the horizon line formed by the compact architecture of the skyscrapers in the city center. The panorama is not unlike that offered by the full expanse of Manhattan, as seen from the western bank of the Hudson River.

West of the Loop that circles Chicago's city center, the industrial city was centered around Goose Island; then, farther to the south along the Sanitary Canal, around the Lake Calumet area; and then farther still, around Gary, Indiana, today a major player in the American iron and steel industry, separated from Chicago by a vast zone of oil refineries and storage facilities. There, on twenty to twenty-five miles of perfectly flat land, the most imposing concentration of industrial activities developed, creating an impressive artificial landscape built by industry. Almost all the components of that environment are of human manufacture; for a century, they have given off a muffled din and

streams of smoke. It is a graphic landscape, marked by hundreds of smokestacks and distillation towers; by a jumble of waterways, train tracks, roads, highways, electric power lines, and gas lines; and by hundreds of acres of large metal buildings arranged in rows, as well as oil depots filled with huge tanks.

In short, it is now a historic landscape—even though it is very far from becoming inactive—and its power to give expression to the industrial age will never be matched by the buildings of high-tech architecture surrounded by manicured lawns, which, in other regions, now house new technology industries and research departments. The more sophisticated the technology, the less obvious the impact of production on our landscapes, except perhaps in the case of the enormous structures that house the assembly of the largest airplanes; but they have little to communicate other than an impression of scale. Conversely, the structures bequeathed by the previous generations of industry and technology still have the merit of making function and process more intelligible, even if they require interpretation.

On Goose Island, now under reconstruction and renamed the Chicago Industrial Corridor, fans of industrial archaeology find ample reason to feel satisfaction. The water surrounding the island is traversed by metal drawbridges, all built on an identical model. Although it is now almost impossible to find concrete traces of the area's slaughterhouses, where tens of thousands of animals from the ranches of the Midwest converged on a daily basis, the city's major role in that enterprise remains intelligible.

In Buffalo, the functional harmony between the waterways of Lake Erie and the Buffalo River and the concentration of steel and concrete grain elevators gave rise to an extraordinary collection of monumental objects, whose skyline brings to mind a high-rise urban district. In 1986, the Preservation Coalition of Erie County, a citizens' pressure group, was formed with the aim to create the Joseph Dart Historic District (named for the inventor of the grain elevator) around that legacy. These grain elevators are both threatened and protected at the same time: threatened by the route of a planned highway, in spite of their relatively

Left: *Bethlehem, Pennsylvania, in 1830 (drawing by George Lehman).*

Below: *The Cambria Iron Works in Johnstown, Pennsylvania, in about 1860.*

Top: *The steel works in Bethlehem, Pennsylvania, in 1907 (drawing by Richard Rummell).*

Left: *The city of Chicago, between Lake Michigan and the industrial zone.*

Above: *A railroad terminal close to Chicago's downtown.*

Above: *Abandoned concrete grain elevators in Buffalo, New York.*

Right: *The grain elevator district of Buffalo. Duluth, the major port on Lake Superior for transporting grain, iron ore, and coal, also possesses a rich heritage of grain elevators, as does Minneapolis.*

233

Above: *The old sugar refinery on the property of Estate Reef Bay, in St. John, the Virgin Islands.*

Right: *A former industrial site in Homestead, Pennsylvania, in the Pittsburgh industrial basin, awaits redevelopment.*

Opposite: *The evaporators for recuperating glycerol at the Colgate factory in Jersey City, New Jersey (photograph taken during demolition).*

PRIVATE PROPERTY NO TRESPASSING

Above: *U.S. Steel foundries Nos. 2, 3, and 4 in Duquesne, Pennsylvania, during demolition in 1993: a spectacular episode in the dismantling of the powerful Pittsburgh industrial basin.*

Left: *The same site in 1998: the last "survivors" in the industrial wasteland.*

Opposite, top: *The defunct Rising & Nelson slate quarries, in the Appalachian region of New England, have been abandoned and invaded by water, producing an artificial landscape.*

Opposite, bottom left: *An industrial wasteland in McKeesport, Pennsylvania.*

Opposite, bottom right: *On the same site, beautiful brick shops bear witness to former prosperity.*

Bethlehem, Pennsylvania, after the shutdown of the steel mills.

Above: *Shops and blast furnaces.*

Right: *Steel conveyors.*

marginal location; and protected by the high price it would cost to demolish them.

Any structure can be destroyed, and the industrial landscape is particularly vulnerable to destruction, on the grounds that its buildings and structures have ceased to be useful or have become a nuisance. We can only regret this eventuality. The understanding and interpretation of a landscape are linked to the preservation of its material landmarks, the irreplaceable artifacts of memory. These landmarks as a whole constitute another way of deciphering history. But is it even possible to preserve the intelligibility of an entire industrial landscape? That question is addressed not only to historians but also to specialists in space management, too many of whom are still undoubtedly fond of starting over from scratch rather than adapting existing structures to current needs. The protection of the heritage requires that more creative solutions be found.

FROM LANDSCAPE TO WASTELAND

The line is quickly crossed between the living industrial landscape and the industrial wasteland, dramatic in its immobility, its abandonment, and its gradual degradation. A professor and photographer at the Illinois Institute of Technology in Chicago has expressed that transition very forcefully: "America," he writes, "moves at such a pace that we repress history. We rushed onto our territory like a lion delighting in its prey. From the beginning, we ran for the horizon, building, rebuilding, discarding. From one end of America to the other, we left behind us, like carcasses after the feast, what had been the latest invention just the day before. Our land is covered with debris that, in a culture other than our own, would be called the ruins of a civilization that must have flourished a thousand years ago, and not just one or two generations back."

In fact, this empty wasteland provides valuable evidence of the industrial heritage and the landscapes it created. It is an essential area for the practice of industrial archaeology, and it calls for further documentation and historical research.

Industrial wastelands raise questions that have no easy answers. They are disturbing because the communities on which they impose their presence do not like disorder and abandonment, and they rightfully do not want ruins on their landscape. The industrial relics are scorned as evidence of the failures of an economic system and of the damage, easily imputed to industry, inflicted on society and the environment. For example, the concentration of oil-refining and chemical industries along the Mississippi River between New Orleans and Baton Rouge was nicknamed "cancer alley," due to the health hazards posed by the emissions that are produced by these industries.

As a result, the problem of industrial wastelands tends to be solved quite simply and swiftly by having them eliminated. Obstacles to their being recycled or preserved cannot be overcome except with time. These obstacles arise particularly as a result of the need to clean up the sites, a process closely controlled by legislation in many states, but also because of unfavorable economic or urban circumstances.

INDUSTRIAL WASTELANDS, A SUBJECT OF DEBATE AND AN OBJECT OF FASCINATION

The protection, preservation, and reuse of the large mining, iron and steel, and metallurgical sites are especially problematic. This is a vast heritage, but also one that is baffling to nonspecialists because the technical nature of the complex machinery and equipment associated with this heritage makes it difficult to decipher. However, the most challenging problem is still how to grapple with pollution and cleanup. The negative reactions of the local population, the considerable delay and high cost of restoring the soil, and the depreciation of the capital represented by the land are a number of the handicaps that hinder the adoption of positive solutions.

Industries and the pollution of the environment that they cause do not constitute a new problem. In the United States, the lure of profit spawned by the discovery of massive resources led, in the nineteenth century, to a brutal exploitation of nature, accompanied by a lack of respect for the ecological balance. An early example is the drilling of petroleum deposits in western Pennsylvania, around 1860. The first crude-oil refinery originated

Above: *The Michigan Central Railroad Station in Detroit stands alone in the middle of a wasteland.*

Left: *The floor in an abandoned Ford factory in Edgewater, New Jersey, bears marks where the machines were once located.*

Above: *The shops of the Central Georgia Railroad in Savannah, dating from the 1850s to 1920, were reduced to ruins prior to their rehabilitation.*

Left: *An old textile factory in the Johns Falls Valley industrial zone of Baltimore.*

in Titusville in 1861; it produced naphtha, lamp oil, and heavy oil, a lubricant containing paraffin. But forty percent of the crude was discarded as waste; it was emptied into Oil Creek or allowed to seep into the soil. In the processing of the lamp oil, sulfuric acid was used to purify and deodorize it, before the oil was washed in a solution of hot caustic soda. In 1863, sixty-one plants of this type were operating in a production region that, to be sure, extended over several counties. The boom towns that grew up around the drilling sites were established on cleared forest land, in a sort of permanent sea of mud.

A century and a half later, a mining region in the West left behind the bleakest ruins: these are the copper mines of Butte-Anaconda in Montana, where the predicted cost of cleanup has also reached record levels. From 1887 to 1950, Butte produced a third of the copper in the United States and a sixth of the copper in the world. The industrial empire built by the Anaconda Copper Mining Corporation (Anaconda is about twenty-five miles to the west), following Marcus Daly's 1898 discovery of the richest vein in the world, dominated the state's economy and political life for seventy-five years and led the world in the production and technology of copper extraction, refining, and metallurgy. In Butte, the mine was very close to the center of the city. It was the setting chosen by Dashiell Hammett for his first novel, *Red Harvest* (1929), in which he describes Butte as "a gray and hideous place, sullied by the mining and refining of ore."

In the past, these refining plants constituted an almost unbearable source of pollution, both from the emissions of the smokestacks and from the waste they left behind, enormous artificial hills of slag piled up in the hope that it could be reprocessed in the future. Even today, huge dumps extending over several square miles contain not only heavy metals (copper, manganese, zinc), but also metal objects from a century of uninterrupted industrial activity. These byproducts are blamed for the contamination of the springs on one entire side of the Columbia River Basin and for the pollution of about sixty miles of waterways.

Over a surface of twenty-five hundred acres, the subsoil, with miles of galleries bored into it, raises the dangerous problem of subsidence. At the site of the Berkeley shaft, after the underground drilling ended and the water was pumped out, a 950-foot-deep toxic lake of acidic water containing heavy metals formed. There, in November 1995, 342 snow geese perished during their migration.

The copper foundries of Anaconda closed in 1980. In 1983, the site was declared a priority on the list of sites to be cleaned up by the Environmental Protection Agency. To aid in the economic reconversion of the area, the notion of industrial heritage has made inroads. A park museum project linking Butte and Anaconda—the Anaconda Historical Park System—was established, and the main interpretive center was set up in the buildings of the Anselmo mine to explain all the surface operations. In 1998, on the site of the old blast furnaces, an eighteen-hole golf course was built.

Nevertheless, industrial wastelands also possess a certain kind of beauty as landscapes of ruins, and the devotees of such landscapes are often the best defenders of the industrial heritage. For the last ten years or so, they have awakened keen interest in a new generation of American photographers, who have been inspired by an acute sense of the industrial aesthetic, and by a desire to emphasize the neoromantic aspect of the ruins, their almost monstrous appearance, and the attraction that emanates from seemingly incomprehensible objects.

In an exhibit of color photographs at Dartmouth College in the 1980s, Serge Hambourg extolled the still almost bucolic charm of the New England textile factories, set amid a forest setting and reflecting in the adjacent rivers. He captured an environment in which industry seemed benign. A radical departure is evident in his work of the 1990s: the photographs, in harsh black and white, focused on the most barren aspects of the industrial heritage of the United States. The photographs no longer expressed the message, "See how beautiful this is." Instead, they brought attention to the technological sophistication of the

American industrial legacy and its role in making the country the foremost global power. The images seemed to carry a new message: "Do not bury the signs of success."

In Duquesne in 1993, photographer Sandy Noyes captured the ovens of U.S. Steel in the process of being razed and demolished. He caught a tragic moment in the history of that steel works, in which the destruction of a particular set of equipment made the totality of the production process unintelligible, but the photographs of the plants retained an extraordinary expressive power. The same artist focused on the scars left on the earth by the exploitation of the slate quarries in New York and Vermont. The open pits remaining after the extraction of the stone ended had filled with water, which reflected the sky and woods. He also captured the defunct open-pit copper ore operations in Montana.

Just north of Duquesne, in McKeesport, Pennsylvania—also known as "Tube City"—photographers have been drawn to the shut-down buildings of a large metallurgical operation from the early twentieth century. The workshops and sheds, large rolling mills, and skeletons of half-demolished ovens appear in photographs as if frozen in time.

In Bethlehem, photographer Joseph Elliott documented the assets of the large Bethlehem Steel plant shortly before its demise. All the components of the production apparatus, observed within and around the buildings of the factory, are represented with a mixture of exactitude and artistic expression, showing Elliott's desire to evoke the meaning behind the stilled equipment.

The assembly floor of a Ford factory in New Jersey attracted photographer Gerald Weinstein's attention, not only for its skeleton of light steel columns but also for the evidence left behind by the machines (taken apart, or perhaps vandalized), echoing traces that almost suggest the footprints of the workers. Closer to New York, he photographed the shops of the large Colgate soap factory before they were demolished, capturing the monumentality of the crisscrossing towers and conveyors, the tanks, and the evaporators clad in their pipes.

No less dramatic are the large urban industrial wastelands, entire districts destroyed by crises of all kinds, which demonstrate the incapacity of the authorities to either erase these ruins or reclaim them. In Detroit, tourists who visit the concrete, steel, and glass towers of the Renaissance Center can take in the panorama to the north, along the Detroit River, of the old industrial port area, where flat, vacant lots occupying the sites of former factories have been transformed into parking lots. To the south, the old industrial zone has disappeared, although one architectural monolith from the 1920s is left standing: the Detroit train station. While awaiting a decision it continues to deteriorate, a process accelerated by the presence of squatters and water damage. But what a dazzling architectural lesson on the exterior, with its projecting section—inspired by Grand Central Station in New York—and its office building, which is in harmony with the architecture of the old city center, built in the time of Detroit's splendor. Its isolation, in the midst of increasing leveled areas, expresses the difficulty that the city has had staying ahead of the speculative initiatives of developers while it makes decisions regarding the reuse of an industrial landmark. To the north, in Highland Park—once the heart of the automobile industry—the vast spaces abandoned by the industry alternate with devastated urban zones awaiting revitalization and reuse.

Fortunately, not all elements of the country's industrial heritage have fallen into a state of ruin. The smaller sites and structures have a greater chance of growing old without being replaced by new, speculative undertakings, being adaptively renovated and reused, or being restored on the basis of aesthetic criteria. But for now, an old sugar factory in the natural tropical setting of the Virgin Islands appears fixed in its role as an attractive ruin, braving the assaults of the climate. Under the mild sky of Georgia, a monumental smokestack and storage tank, previously part of the shops of the Central Georgia Railroad in

Savannah, look like brick and cast-iron artworks. In Baltimore's architectural and industrial heritage corridor, the Johns Falls Valley, a mid-nineteenth century textile factory with an Italianate style gable and an elaborate polygonal chimney has become a warehouse; it is poorly maintained, but may yet know better days.

Fortunately, private and public initiatives in the last thirty years have led to a shift in priorities, from concern for the most appealing objects to an appreciation of the large complexes, which, in the end, are the most representative of the bygone phases of industrialization.

CHAPTER 7

Rehabilitation, Preservation, Reuse

The gradual dawning of the country's sensitivity to the cultural significance and value of its technical and industrial heritage owes a great deal to the role played by engineers. They were not only the creators of that heritage, as we have seen in the previous chapters, but also the initiators of the policy for preserving the evidence of the technical ingenuity that characterized the industrial history of the United States. That policy has developed with the support of certain institutions and professional associations.

A MOVEMENT TAKES FORM: FROM THE TECHNICAL COLLECTIONS TO ENGINEERS' ASSOCIATIONS

Following the 1876 centennial exposition in Philadelphia, the Smithsonian Institution received all the technological objects in trust. G. Brown Goode, the curator charged with managing the new collection, then outlined a plan for a department of technology. Up until that point, the museum had been primarily devoted to the subjects of natural history and anthropology. Goode even envisioned a national museum of technology and industry that would be the center of a network of museums distributed throughout the United States.

The Smithsonian is a remarkable institution with an interesting history. The library was the original nucleus of what has become an astounding collection, whose headquarters still stands on the Mall in Washington, D.C. It originated with the bequest of James Smithson (1765–1829), the illegitimate but acknowledged son of the Duke of Northumberland and himself a great chemist and naturalist, who left his entire fortune to the United States government in an act of spite against England. That fortune, equivalent to one-and-a-half times the federal budget of the period, was earmarked "for the growth and diffusion of knowledge in the world." As of today, it has produced seventeen specialized museums and now primarily supports scientific research.

The 1905 Bellows Falls Bridge in Vermont, with its distinctive metal-frame arch and suspension cables.

Goode's successors, John Elfreth Watkins (1852–1903), former engineer of the Pennsylvania Railroad and author of *The Beginnings of Engineering* (1891), and George Colton Maynard (1839–1918), engineer of the telegraph and telephone system, also did a great deal to build collections of technological objects. In about 1920, these collections were already among the richest in the world. After these curators, the mining engineer Carl W. Nitman further extended their activities, and, in 1920, he was the first to call for the creation of a national museum of technology and industry, or a museum of engineering, similar to the large institutions already established in Europe: the South Kensington Museum in London, the Conservatoire National des Arts et Métiers in Paris, and the Deutsches Museum in Munich. His mission anticipated the discourse of the current defenders of the industrial heritage. Along with his colleague, the mechanical engineer Holbrook Fitz-John Porter, Nitman launched a fundraising campaign, supported by the four major engineering associations and by the *New York Times*. He based his arguments on the notion that such a museum would foster national pride.

But the two men collected only ten thousand dollars. Even with the example set by Henry Ford, who created his own museum in Dearborn, Michigan, industrialists generally preferred to finance museums of fine art rather than technical ones; or, they focused on preserving the heritage of the colonial period, or at least the era prior to the Civil War. Hence, in the 1930s, Ford and John D. Rockefeller financed the restoration of Colonial Williamsburg, in Virginia. The 1929 stock-market crash put an end to Nitman's plan, but the idea was reborn after World War II. Frank Taylor, a disciple of Nitman's, relaunched the plan, and Congress set up a grant for the creation of a Museum of History and Technology, which opened in 1964 on the Washington Mall, next to the Smithsonian Institution. Its broad conception encompassed both the presentation of American science and technology and that of political, cultural, and social life. As a result, in 1980, the museum was renamed the National Museum of American History. Through the efforts of its department heads and researchers, such as Robert Vogel and Helena Smith, it was the birthplace, in the early 1970s, of the Society of Industrial Archaeology.

The origin and growth of that organization owed a great deal to the actions of professional associations of engineers—such as the American Society of Civil Engineers, the American Society of Mechanical Engineers, the Institute of Electrical and Electronics Engineers, and the Public Works Historical Society—who were preoccupied at the time with focusing the attention of their own members, as well as that of the general public, on the history of great American achievements. Together they gave their support to the creation, contemporaneous with that of the Society of Industrial Archaeology, of a federal inventory and study program within the National Park Service, under the authority of the Department of the Interior and with the cooperation of the Library of Congress. This was the Historic American Engineering Record (HAER), whose documentation, accumulated over the last thirty years by skilled teams, has played a large role in the preparation of this book.

THE EARLY REHABILITATION OF INDUSTRIAL MONUMENTS

The 1960s witnessed the arrival of the first practitioners in the movement to preserve, rehabilitate, and reuse industrial buildings. These were inspired speculators, architects, city officials, and citizens' associations. The economic recession of the 1970s also played a role, providing surrendered ground for the architects' initiatives.

The first experiment of the industrial heritage movement was Ghirardelli Square in San Francisco, between 1964 and 1968. Domenico Ghirardelli was a Genoa candy maker who settled in among the California gold prospectors in 1849, and then moved to San Francisco where, in 1867, he perfected a process for crushing cacao beans with a millstone, which earned him his celebrity. In 1893, his sons chose an old wool factory for their chocolate operation, located in the northern section of the waterfront. In the early years of the twentieth century, they added brick buildings with crenelations and ornaments in molded concrete, including the clock tower building, which was inspired by a late portion of the Château de Blois.

Ghirardelli, enjoying great prosperity, moved again in 1960. Demolition of the buildings might have followed, but in 1962 a family of shipowners showed interest in saving them, with the goal of making the renovation the starting point for a large urban development project. From the beginning, the operation involved a block of buildings rather than one isolated monument. The architects preserved all the facades of the buildings, which were remodeled on the interior to be occupied mostly by apartments with superb views of the bay, and adapted the lower levels for commercial use, such as restaurants and specialized shops. The same architectural firm (Wurster, Bernardi & Emmons) was responsible for the rehabilitation, in 1967–69, of two icehouses brought in from Alaska, built in 1914–15 by the National Ice and Cold Storage Company, which had been founded in 1892.

Elsewhere in the country there were other examples of the reinsertion of industrial buildings with architectural interest into the fabric and life of a large city. The San Antonio Museum of Art, opened in 1981, occupies the buildings of the Lone Star Brewery, one of the most important breweries in Texas, located on the San Antonio River. Built between 1895 and 1904 from the plans of E. Jungerfeld, a St. Louis firm, for the Anheuser-Busch company, the brewery included eight yellow brick buildings in the Italianate style, incorporating cast-iron elements. Closed during Prohibition, it was turned into a cotton-spinning mill and then became the headquarters for a chain of grocery stores. Thereafter, it remained vacant for a long period. The brewery was listed on the National Register of Historic Places, and five of its eight buildings were purchased in 1972 by the San Antonio Museum Association, whose plan obtained public and private financing. The association saw a way to take advantage of the vast interior spaces, which include very high vaulted ceilings and massive walls. Breweries in other locations have also been converted for residential and other uses: for example, the Tivoli Union Brewing Company in Denver, Colorado, and the Hinckel Brewery in Albany, dating from 1880. Another initiative that created a stir for its originality and boldness was the conversion of the Quaker

Oats factory and its grain elevators in Akron, Ohio, into two hundred circular hotel rooms.

Preservationists have become excited about other forms of the industrial heritage. In particular, historic bridges were often the occasion for an offensive on the part of local preservation associations, which opposed the insensitive actions of the departments involved in renovating the road traffic network. In Bellows Falls, Vermont, the metal arch bridge connecting that town to Walpole, New Hampshire, across the Connecticut River, had been closed to all but pedestrian traffic since 1971. The engineering department was resolved to have it destroyed on the grounds it was unsafe. The residents fought for its preservation for five years, managing to mount a national media campaign in December 1982, but were unable to prevent its demolition. (Ironically, the four explosive charges did not completely destroy the bridge, which was said to be so fragile.)

Operations for rehabilitating or reusing train stations also multiplied, targeting buildings from the turn of the twentieth century that offered both technological and aesthetic interest. The central offices of the Pittsburgh and Lake Erie Railroad were installed in Pittsburgh, Pennsylvania, in 1879; the line was designed to revitalize the coal, coke, and iron ore industry of that city. In 1898–1901, the company decided to add a large passenger train station, designed by the architect William George Burns. Behind the massive, classical facade, no effort was spared to ensure the splendor of the interior, outfitted in marble, copper, wood, and glass. The large waiting hall has been converted into a luxury restaurant, and the old covered train platforms have been transformed into a shopping center with about one hundred shops; adjacent is a small open-air museum dedicated to the rolling stock and to an authentic Bessemer converter, a symbol of the history of iron and steel in the Monongahela Valley. The conversion was conducted by the Pittsburgh History and Landmarks Foundation, formed in 1964. The entire complex has been listed on the National Register of Historic Places.

Union Station in St. Louis, Missouri, dating from 1894, has the largest glass railroad shed in the United States. It was convert-ed in the 1980s into a hotel complex and shopping center. Its counterpart in Albany, New York, dating from 1903, was built for the New York Central and Hudson River Railroad. The granite structure was designed in the Beaux Arts style by Shepley, Rutan & Coolidge of Boston, successors to prominent architect Henry Hobson Richardson. The station closed in 1968; in 1984, it was finally purchased by Norstar Bancorp, and became the Norstar Plaza. In contrast, the train station in Tacoma, Washington, built in 1911 for the Northern Pacific, the Union Pacific, and the Great Northern railroads, was occupied by federal administration offices after being abandoned by Amtrak. The citizens' group Save Our Station successfully opposed a plan to convert it into a commercial center.

Adaptive reuse also occurred early on in several large-scale projects in the South. A case in point is the Sloss Furnaces, whose rescue is discussed below. In Savannah, Georgia, the repair shops of the Central Georgia Railroad were converted into a multiple-use complex in 1980. In Richmond, Virginia, along the James River, the Tredegar Ironworks complex, a weapons and munitions factory during the Confederacy, was converted into the Riverside Museum.

EARLY URBAN INDUSTRIAL DISTRICTS

In the 1970s, the concept emerged of reinserting large industrial complexes—as opposed to isolated monuments—into urban redevelopment plans, in the form of cultural parks. These experiments took place particularly in New England, where the textile factories that had dominated a number of small and mid-sized cities in the nineteenth century became the focus of heritage preservation. Certain sites have taken on a particular patriotic significance as the birthplace of American industrialization, which is viewed as synonymous with national independence, as it helped to emancipate the country from the economic control of England.

Preservation of the industrial heritage benefited from the tax measures introduced by the Tax Reform Act of 1976. The

The anchorage of the metal arch of the Bellows Falls Bridge.

Above: *An open-air museum around the Pittsburgh train station displays this Bessemer converter, which evokes the past glory of the local iron and steel industry.*

Right: *The renovated train station at the center of Station Square in Pittsburgh.*

Top: *Established in 1835 and closed in 1954, Boott Mills in Lowell, Massachusetts, currently houses a historical and technological museum in its building No. 6 (dating from the 1870s). A cotton-weaving shop containing eighty-eight looms is used for demonstrations. The shop re-creates the work atmosphere of the 1920s.*

Above right: *A renovated factory from the early twentieth century now houses the Museum of American Textile History. Established in North Andover, Massachusetts, in 1960, the museum was moved to Lowell in 1997, under the directorship of Paul Rivard.*

Above left: *A residential complex has been developed in Lowell's old Massachusetts Mills.*

Opposite: *A pedestrian zone known as Market Place was created at the heart of Lowell's former factory district; it houses the visitors center.*

intention of the legislation was to discourage the demolition of historic buildings by making the option of rehabilitation competitive with new construction. In order to receive the benefits of these rehabilitation efforts, projects had to be certified to meet the standards defined by the offices for archaeology and heritage protection in the Department of the Interior. The administration defined rehabilitation as a process of returning a property to usable condition, either by repairing or by modifying it, with the condition that a future reuse would be compatible with the preservation of those parts or characteristics of the property that had a historic, architectural, or cultural value, and that the alterations in the property would not be irreversible. Clearly, the emphasis was placed on respect for a historic heritage.

That is what convinced the HAER to begin, in 1977, several model rehabilitation projects in a few industrial cities in the South: Lynchburg, Virginia; Winston-Salem and Spencer, North Carolina; and Columbus, Georgia. In Columbus, in particular, the initiative was well received by the local authorities, who had already undertaken to rehabilitate the city's former metallurgical plants.

In this new context, the preservationists could more comfortably develop an argument that would demonstrate to their clients the advantages of plans that respect the integrity of historic architecture. Investment savings could reach up to thirty percent, compared to the cost of new construction (especially if there is a possibility of reusing the preexisting technological infrastructure); the greater the speed of execution, the greater the correlative savings in energy and natural resources. Thus, urban sprawl could be slowed, a broad range of job opportunities could be created, the urban heritage could be celebrated, and the legacy of the industrial age could be respected. The HAER team rightfully insisted that the success of such rehabilitation operations was dependent on the establishment of cooperation between local authorities, private individuals, architects, planners, and leading preservationists.

The first American city to benefit from systematic industrial development, though at a relatively modest scale, was Pater-

son, New Jersey. It was also the first city to obtain the recognition, from President Gerald Ford in 1976, of a national industrial historic district that covered 120 acres. In about 1965, a municipal urban renewal plan was conceived around the Rogers Locomotive Works; it threatened to destroy—in favor of a highway—the canal system and about forty factories still in operation. The project was scrapped as a result of the actions of a citizens' group headed by Mary Ellen Kramer. The Great Falls Historic District was set in place by her husband, Lawrence F. Kramer, who became the mayor. The 1914 hydroelectric plant, located below the falls, was renovated and again began to produce energy for the city. In 1982 Raceway Park opened, a wooded recreation area centered around the reconstruction of two-thirds of the hydraulic system feeding the old factories. Federal funds were supposed to support a model development project for a new downtown, incorporating retail use, housing, artists' studios, and industrial activities. But a change in the city administration threatened the industrial district, which was left to languish; squatters caused fires in several former factories. Finally, in the 1980s, a new project focused on the development of low-cost housing permitted the conversion-rehabilitation of two silk factories, Essex Mill and Phenix Mill.

Lowell, Massachusetts, once an industrial center of much larger dimensions (100,000 residents in 1900), had been in a state of decline since the 1920s. The urban renewal operations undertaken in that city beginning in 1950 destroyed entire neighborhoods. The industrial past was not getting good press; people still had a tendency to speak of "satanic mills," and the order of the day was less to preserve the heritage than to start again from scratch.

Although many of the most interesting factories and workers' housing from the first decades of industrialization had already been obliterated by urban renewal, Patrick Mogan, a former school principal who became director of city planning, relied on the Federal Model Cities Program of 1966 in his decision to develop a vast plan for transforming the obsolete factory district into a national historic park. In 1978, Washington granted

Lowell the status Mogan had desired, in addition to 9 million dollars in federal aid: the city was designated the most representative industrial community in the United States.

In great part, it was thanks to the efforts of the late senator Paul Tsongas, himself a native of Lowell, that the federal law had been passed. A member of the city council since 1969, Tsongas remained until his death the coach for the city's administrative team. Governor Michael Dukakis also supported the creation of Lowell Heritage State Park. An enormous open-air museum traversed by a six-mile hydraulic network whose canals, dams, and locks had remained nearly intact, Lowell was able to enjoy a revitalization of its economy. There, much more than in Paterson, the principle of revitalizing the industrial zones in decline prevailed, thanks to a thoughtful rehabilitation plan and the cooperation between federal, state, and local governments. Lowell became a tourist attraction; a new stadium, a Hilton Hotel, restaurants, and fourteen new schools were built, and thousands of jobs were created. All the same, a certain tension has arisen among local institutions regarding the spirit of the site's development—among the academic culture (the university, the Tsongas Industrial History Center founded in 1987, the archives, and the museums) and the more popular or traditional groups (Lowell has had its own historical society since the nineteenth century), not to mention the interpretation of history given by the staff of the National Park Service.

Boston is the financial capital of New England, but it was only remotely linked to the large textile region nearby. That city also carried out a large-scale rehabilitation operation at the Charlestown Navy Yards, whose slips and workshops were active from 1801 to 1974. The yards are historically significant and a source of national pride. The extraordinary architecture of the site is characterized by the austerity of massive rectangular granite buildings from the early nineteenth century and the decorative elegance of large brick buildings from the later part of the same century. The city of Boston and the National Park Service joined forces to reclaim about twenty-five acres of this site, classified as a national historic landmark, including a grid of per-

fectly aligned streets, about twenty buildings, a dry dock, and the *Constitution*, a wood frigate and the oldest ship in the navy; it became the Boston National Historic Park. The buildings were converted one by one into museums, luxury homes, offices, and businesses. In this case, the protection of the industrial heritage was behind a true urban redevelopment project: new apartments and bungalows blend harmoniously with the historic buildings, and the yacht port is a sort of replica of the large dry dock that has been preserved. The area is entered through the original gates to the military and industrial site.

The case of other northeastern cities is rather different. The textile-industry cities of Manchester, New Hampshire, and Lawrence, Massachusetts, despite the imposing nature of the buildings they have preserved and the efforts to develop other state urban parks nearby, offer no comparable examples of urban organization associated with the concentration of factories in a homogeneous district.

As for ports, New York City allowed its port zone extending along Manhattan's West Side to disappear almost entirely, and it has been slow to address the fate of other areas of industrial waterfront development, such as the warehouses in Red Hook and the Brooklyn Navy Yard. However, the city has paid tribute to industrial archaeology in the remarkable efforts to preserve the architecture of the SoHo-Cast Iron Historic District, which is a remarkably intact concentration of nineteenth-century cast-iron-fronted loft buildings, as well as the warehouses and factory buildings in the four Tribeca Historic Districts. Many of these buildings have been converted for use as residential lofts, galleries, offices, retail stores, and restaurants, breathing new life into these neighborhoods.

In Philadelphia, which has an impressive industrial zone along its waterfront, the celebration of the industrial heritage has manifested itself only marginally, in the maintenance of the Fairmount Waterworks park. Located on the west bank of the Schuylkill River and built in 1812, this complex of neoclassical temple-fronted structures masked their utilitarian function: they housed pumping facilities, driven by hydraulic energy, that were

Top and bottom: *The Charlestown Navy Yards in Boston, Massachusetts.*

Opposite, top: *The preservation of a Boston dry dock.*

Opposite, bottom left: *The former labor exchange of the old navy yard.*

Opposite, bottom right: *A museum devoted to the history of the navy in one of the oldest of the Charlestown shipyard buildings. The* Constitution, *the oldest American warship still afloat, was restored in Boston in 1992.*

Top: *The Days Inn hotel chain has taken over a renovated factory in Baltimore.*

Above: *Marlboro Square, luxury lofts in a former clothing factory.*

Right: *The Fairmount Waterworks in Philadelphia were once the water-pumping facilities for the city.*

Top: *The Mount Clare locomotive roundhouse of the B&O Railroad was rehabilitated and converted into a museum.*

Left: *The architecture of Baltimore's Camden Station has been beautifully restored. The rehabilitation of the station and the imposing warehouse has played a pivotal role in the urban redevelopment project of the harbor area.*

Top: *The large B&O warehouse.*

Above left: *Westport Station (1906), an imposing thermal power station at Baltimore's Inner Harbor, has been converted into a venue for rock music. In about 1987, some considered establishing a national museum of electricity on the site. All the internal equipment has been preserved intact.*

Above right: *One wing of Camden Station has been converted into a sports museum, an adjunct to the new commercial and sports center.*

designed to improve Philadelphia's water supply. Defunct since before 1920, these facilities were popular attractions in the nineteenth century, a favorite place for Philadelphians and out-of-towners alike to go for strolls. In 1976, the site was declared a national historic landmark. Having once more become a recreation area, the site also preserves some of its original equipment.

In contrast to Philadelphia, Baltimore—one of the country's historic cities with a rich industrial heritage—has for the last two decades applied an effective policy for reintegrating that heritage into the life of the city, which unfortunately had been dispossessed of a significant part of its economic assets. That reintegration has come about in several phases. One phase involved the rehabilitation of the port areas, divided into two very distinct sites: Inner Harbor and Fells Point. At the former, the work consisted of developing the immediate approaches to the harbor with new facilities designed to revitalize the port, making it a site for commercial and recreational activities. Hotels, restaurants, banks, and insurance company buildings appeared, along with a world-class aquarium and luxury homes with a direct view of the port, the configuration of which retains its charm. The new development was balanced by the protection, rehabilitation, and recuperation of a certain number of buildings that are significant to the industrial and maritime heritage. These are of exceptional quality: thermal power stations, a vertical tower, warehouses, and old factories once clustered around the railroad and the seaway. The complex now constitutes a historic district, where it is still possible to imagine what the commercial and manufacturing life was like in a large port. At the southern mouth of Inner Harbor, near the Domino Sugar refinery, an 1865 cannery was adapted to house the Baltimore Museum of Industry. Departments in the museum are devoted to the most remarkable activities of local industry, from the mussel cannery in the Chesapeake Bay to an unexpected range of products for everyday life produced by the sheet-metal industry. An educational service, supported by the National Endowment for the Humanities, welcomes children from the schools of Baltimore County, who visit the reconstituted workshops and learn about the deeds of their ancestors. A library and archive service supports cultural research. One of the results has been an inventory of the county's industrial heritage.

Other efforts in Baltimore were devoted to extolling the memory of the Baltimore & Ohio, the most glorious of the American railroad companies in the early phases of expansion into western territory. The old roundhouse was transformed into a railroad museum, from which tours on real trains depart; the nearby locomotive construction shop, dating from the mid-nineteenth century, is awaiting restoration. A master stroke was achieved with the restoration of the Camden Station and of an imposing warehouse that towers over the railroad tracks. That project has brought back to life an urban zone now centered around the baseball stadium for the Baltimore Orioles.

Finally, in the old textile zone (the Johns Falls River Valley), the preservation of Mount Vernon Mills No. 1, which still houses businesses, and the rehabilitation and reuse of Mount Vernon Mills No. 2, converted into a "Mill Centre" and occupied by many tertiary activities, also represent successes. As these various examples in Baltimore demonstrate, the incorporation of the industrial heritage into present-day culture is without a doubt a pertinent initiative.

THE CONCEPT OF THE HERITAGE CORRIDOR

The *heritage corridor* is a geographical area possessing a clearly determined industrial identity. It is dotted with numerous structures that form a network of landmarks and evoke the old industrial landscape.

The first national heritage corridor was created in 1984. It spans 290,000 acres in the region of the Illinois & Michigan Canal, a waterway ninety-five miles long, built between 1836 and 1848 between the Chicago River and La Salle, on the Illinois River. This was the last canal built during the heyday when canals constituted the country's highways. After successfully resisting competition from the railroad and experiencing its highest level of traffic in 1882, it gradually had to give way to the proliferation of roads converging toward Chicago. Abandoned in 1933 upon the opening of the Illinois Waterway, a more modern thoroughfare,

Building No. 2 of the Mount Vernon Mills in the Johns Falls Valley in Baltimore, renamed "Mill Centre," was converted into offices. In the late nineteenth century, the company absorbed the Meadow Mill Company, another cotton-duck weaving business, which owned fourteen factories, some of them located outside Maryland, and which thrived until about 1915.

Top: *A large textile factory in Woonsocket, Rhode Island, has been rehabilitated into a residential district.*

Left: *In Pawtucket, Rhode Island, the Slater Mill has been restored and converted into a museum.*

Above left: *A shopping plaza now occupies the site of a portion of the Ford factories in Detroit's Highland Park.*

Above right: *The large Uniroyal tire factory on the banks of the Detroit River was demolished in 1986, but this roadside advertising relic continues to serve as a reminder to motorists alongside a highway.*

Opposite: *A 1920s factory in the center of Detroit awaits rescue.*

the Illinois & Michigan Canal largely contributed to Chicago's expansion into the economic capital of the Midwest, as well as opened up the whole region to growth and commerce. The Illinois & Michigan Canal Heritage Corridor is a new version of the national park; it combines trails, historic and even prehistoric sites, small riverside towns along the canal, and rural, mining, and manufacturing landscapes—not to mention technical achievements linked to the canal itself. There, the preservation of both the heritage and the environment is directed toward an economic revitalization of the region.

In Rhode Island, on the outskirts of Providence, a similar project celebrating the industrial heritage has developed: the Blackstone River Valley Heritage Corridor. The starting point for the establishment of the corridor was the Slater Mill—now preserved, developed, and transformed into a museum—an extremely important site venerated as a symbol of national independence. A research and interpretive center serves as a gateway to the river itself, which can now be enjoyed once again, thanks to the skillful redevelopment of its banks and a boat-tour program. Farther away from the city, the landmarks of the previous century's industrialization abound (dams controlling the falls, a side canal, and factories); these landmarks within the heritage corridor are being carefully rehabilitated and signposts discreetly installed.

SETBACKS IN PRESERVATION

Despite many triumphs, the industrial heritage has never won the game in advance, even in New England, which received early attention from researchers and archaeologists. Beginning in 1971, the New England Textile Mills Survey carried out by the Historic Architectural Buildings Survey (HABS), the agency that spawned the HAER, put together an inventory model. In the 1980s, the *Newsletter of the American Society of Industrial Archaeology* gave a significant place to the catastrophes that have continued to destroy some of the treasures of the industrial heritage. The cause is almost always fire, whether intentional or accidental.

Between 1880 and 1920, Fall River, Massachusetts, was one of the largest centers for cotton mills in the western hemisphere. The city is also known for the formidable granite architecture of its factories. One of these factories, the Tecumseh Cotton Mill, was rehabilitated to house the elderly in 125 apartments, yet another example of a successful residential conversion. Unfortunately, another factory in Fall River was destroyed by fire in November 1982; and in 1987, the six-story brick Kerr Thread Mill, formerly the property of American Thread, also went up in flames.

In Lowell, in March 1987, there was a fire at the Lawrence Manufacturing Company, one of the major old companies, dating from 1832. One of these buildings had a superb facade framed by two six-story stairwells. The walls collapsed under the intense heat because the sprinklers had been shut off to keep the pipes from freezing. In Lowell, only three of the original nine companies are still active: Boott, Massachusetts, and Suffolk.

Lynn, Massachusetts, just north of Boston, was once one of the largest global centers for shoe production, a leader in the adoption of an industrial system for shoemaking and in the use of the sewing machine. Many shoe factories survived into the early 1980s, and then began to undergo renovations for use as offices, stores, and apartments. However, in November 1982, an arson fire that raged for ten hours destroyed seventeen factories and damaged nine others, ravaging seven acres.

Certain factors have contributed to the trend toward leveling obsolete industrial sites: the enormity of the vacant spaces, making them difficult and expensive to convert; the considerable variability in the demand for redevelopment from one place to another; and the disdain for or frank hostility toward the industrial heritage on the part of the public. The destruction of these sites continues unabated.

One of the most spectacular examples of the ravaging of the industrial heritage is offered by the city of Detroit and its vast metropolitan area. Devastated by the race riots that erupted in the late 1960s in the areas near the old nineteenth-century urban core, impoverished by a deep crisis in the automobile industry

The Sloss Furnaces in Birmingham, Alabama. The metallurgical industry in Birmingham took off during the Civil War, when it began to supply armaments to the Confederates, and Jefferson County prospered as a result. The rapid growth of James Withers Sloss's business dates from the 1880s; the first iron pipe was cast in 1890. Successful efforts to preserve the site have made it a model for rehabilitating large industrial sites.

Above and right: *Watkins Glen Mill in Lawson, Missouri, has been converted into a museum. One of the floors still has all its machines in place. This is the finest collection of textile machines preserved on site in North America.*

beginning in the 1970s, deserted by its middle-class population and by the relocation of the automobile industry to other cities in Michigan or to other states, Detroit has become a martyr of the industrial heritage movement. The city government and many of its residents showed a fierce dedication to cleaning up the traces of the past. An article in the *Detroit Free Press* on July 15, 1986, listed, under the headline "The Art of Destruction," all the words describing demolition techniques: "to blast, to smash, to jackhammer."

In 1990, Charles K. Hyde, an attentive historian of industrial archaeology in Michigan and a scholar of Albert Kahn, noted a slowing down in the destructive frenzy and the emergence of a few rehabilitation projects in Detroit. It takes a great deal of imagination, however, to reconstitute from a few large survivors what Highland Park was like in the first half of the twentieth century, when the enormous factories and assembly floors of Packard, Dodge, Chrysler, Fisher, and Ford stood side by side on thousands of acres. Here and there, the occupation of a site by other businesses saves from destruction a few components of the architecture of the automobile industry. Yet, this crucial industry has no museum of its history and technology, even though the Henry Ford Museum, in Dearborn, preserves tens of thousands of photographs and the Detroit Institute of Arts houses Diego Rivera's frescoes from the River Rouge plant. Revolutionary in their inspiration, the murals paradoxically were commissioned by one of the wealthiest capitalists in the country; they celebrate the workers who, with their machines, were responsible for the business's greatness.

Recently, a daring operation for reusing space—if not buildings—has created, at an intersection distinguished by Ford's bank and in close proximity to one of the first Ford office buildings in Highland Park, the Model T Plaza, a huge market in the corner of a large parking lot. This commercial market stands against a background of old workshops, and its internal layout attests to a certain respect for the site it occupies, even though it has been totally removed from its industrial use. The customers are welcomed by a display window featuring a Ford Model T and a small gallery of some of the most famous photographs documenting the factory between the two world wars. In short, the project is a pedagogical effort to reintroduce present-day customers to the memory of one of the most flamboyant episodes of twentieth-century industrial growth.

Nevertheless, a "renaissance"—a word charged with meaning for urban development and for the economy—has had a great deal of trouble materializing in Detroit. Along Jefferson Avenue, the artery heading south along the Detroit River, the industrial wasteland and the mortification of the urban fabric seem to have taken hold—with the disappearance of the countless subcontracting and service activities that the automobile industry always engendered around it—in River Rouge and Highland Park. Outside the city center, the absence of any real revitalization of the industrial heritage is obvious (apart from a few felicitous rehabilitations in the historic port sector), both in the void left by the demolition of the huge Uniroyal factory to the north and, to the south, in the absence of any decision concerning the fate of the old Detroit train station. That station, once a point of entry for hundreds of thousands of black migrants from the Southern states, stands as a lonesome skyscraper in the center of a wasteland. How much longer will it embody the memory of the prosperity that its superb gates seemed to promise to those who passed through them? Finally, although the industrial history begun only in the early years of the twentieth century had run its course by century's end, the resistance to the "demolitionist" frenzy seems to be out of steam in Detroit, a city where the Michigan Department of Environmental Quality recently granted nearly 4 million dollars to aid in "cleaning up" a few more of the oldest Packard, Ford, and Chrysler buildings in Detroit and Dearborn.

GRAIN ELEVATORS: A BURDENSOME HERITAGE

The American cities that experienced prosperity in the grain business, and that have inherited collections of grain elevators as a result, have attempted to preserve this type of industrial memory at little cost—that is, by exploiting them as tourist attractions.

Thus, in Buffalo and Duluth, which possess the finest collections of these monuments, it has become popular to tour the port zone by boat.

In Buffalo, in Inner Harbor and along the Buffalo River, the boat tour passes a series of empty shells in every style, but also operating elevators that serve the malt houses and mills, since Buffalo remains the foremost center in the United States for the production of flour. Perhaps pedestrian and automobile tours will be added some day. However, many plans put forward since the 1980s that aimed to find new uses for the elevators have never been executed.

In Duluth, the impressive panorama of the waterfront of Lake Superior has been the object of a vast conversion project: warehouses and offices have been transformed into stores and restaurants, and a park and an interpretive center focused on the history of the grain trade have been created. Open since 1973, the interpretive center had been visited by 10 million tourists by 1997—that is, more than 400,000 per year. In Duluth as well, between the spring and the fall, tour boats pass by the elevators several times a day, making accessible the story of these enormous structures that facilitated the agricultural development of the Midwest.

Minneapolis has even more ambitious goals. The industrial legacy of General Mills, in particular—distributed over several blocks along the Mississippi River across from the Falls of Saint Anthony and included within the West Side Milling District—will offer not only a large number of diversified uses but also a "mill ruins park," designed to preserve grain elevators that have been partially destroyed.

In other cases, an isolated elevator has served as the pretext for a conversion obviously unrelated to its original use. If it is under the protection of the Department of the Interior, it may nevertheless be subject to the prohibitions regarding any significant structural modification to classified buildings. And yet, how can one avoid cutting openings in the walls of a grain elevator, for example, if one wants to have natural light? In at least two cases, there have been adaptations that have been very popular among users and tourists. The first is the Quaker Hilton in Akron, Ohio.

When the Quaker Oats Cereal Company elevators and factory closed in 1971, a local architect, influenced by the example of the Ghirardelli chocolate factory in San Francisco, decided to turn the buildings into a hotel, a restaurant, and a business and conference center. Quaker Square was placed on the list of national historic buildings in 1977, despite the creation of many windows and the addition of balconies. The second case involves the Minneapolis architect who, shortly after his participation as a consultant in the Akron project, turned a set of fourteen elevators dating from the years 1909–30 into apartments, cutting twelve hundred windows into the walls. The elevators definitively proved that they were so solid in their construction that it was absurd to spend a great deal of money to destroy them.

THE PROBLEM OF LARGE IRON AND STEEL SITES

In Birmingham, Alabama, the enthusiasts of the iron and steel heritage had the chance to save Sloss Furnaces. A site of relatively modest dimensions, it includes two blast furnaces that operated between 1931 and 1971 and a building of compressors dating from 1902. The last owner donated the site to the state of Alabama, suggesting that it could be turned into a museum of industry. The state, after years of delay, and after considering the demolition of the structures to install a theme park in their place, in the end donated them to the city of Birmingham. In the meantime, the site had deteriorated and had suffered from vandalism and pillaging. The city, experiencing the same embarrassment, also considered demolition and the reclamation of the land for other economic and speculative uses. Finally, a civic organization was formed and obtained a referendum from the city regarding the protection, restoration, preservation, and transformation of the site into a museum. The latter fell under the jurisdiction of the municipality, which had to seek additional federal financing (from the National Park Service) or private funding. The referendum passed, and Sloss Furnaces were officially proclaimed a museum of the city of Birmingham in 1983, before being classified as a national historic landmark.

Left: *The Eleutherian Mills in Greenville, Delaware, was Du Pont de Nemour's first factory. The building was converted into a museum of American industrial history, devoted primarily to the Brandywine River Valley.*

Below: *The flatting mill and its waterwheel on the banks of the Brandywine River.*

Opposite, top: *The owner's residence.*

Opposite, bottom: *The Powder House, a mill for manufacturing gunpowder.*

273

Top: *The main facade of the Henry Ford Museum in Dearborn, Michigan.*

Bottom: *The entrance to Greenfield Village, an outdoor museum at the Henry Ford Museum.*

Opposite, top: *The central hall of Dearborn Station in Chicago has been converted to commercial use.*

Opposite, bottom left: *The conversion of a Chicago factory to commercial use.*

Opposite, bottom right: *The central tower of the train station.*

The Sexton Lofts in Chicago, a very successful residential conversion.

THE SEXTON
LOFTS
467-090

After twelve years, the state of the "monument" was rather disastrous: maintaining it would have cost little, but repairing it proved to be ruinously expensive. The municipal administration defined three objectives: reconstitute the manufacturing process in the form of a tour and demonstration, with the help of a small furnace; offer a place for public gatherings; and house a metal arts center. The museum also purchased six workers' houses, which were put on display to emphasize and interpret social themes, such as daily living and working conditions and employee-management relations. The rails were reestablished—the site was initially located at the intersection of two important railroad lines—making it possible to rediscover the connection to other industrial sites in the region. And with the help of a small steam boiler, the mechanical bellows were put back into operation. The museum also became a site for cultural events, such as symphony concerts and the annual Birmingham Jam, which produces three days of gospel, blues, and jazz. That aspect of the conversion has been replicated in Germany, where two major sites of the European iron and steel industry, Duisburg-Meiderich (Rhine-Westphalia) and Völkingen (Saarland), are attempting similar experiments.

The Sloss Furnaces adventure offered a great deal of new technical understanding of the conditions for repairing and maintaining metal structures. The surface of the blast furnaces was scrubbed, vacuum cleaned, coated with a special mastic, and then painted. At first, the furnaces were repainted every four years with red paint, but then another color was chosen, closer to a rust tone, in a paint that ought to last fifteen years. The lighter steel components, such as catwalks, stairways, and platforms, were simply replaced if in too poor a state, for obvious safety reasons. Finally, there was the more difficult problem of protecting the interior of the metal structures—including large pipes, ovens, and tubes circulating steam—which, since they had ceased operation and were left cold, had been attacked by mold and moisture. Hot dry air was blasted into them. The smokestacks were all closed at the top to prevent water from falling into them and filling the tunnels that once served as channels for the smoke. For the time being, this is a unique case in the United States, and it raises the question of whether or not we have the luxury in this country of saving several sites of this type.

In 1997, at the defunct Bethlehem Steel Company, a plan as daring as it was appealing was formulated: following a coordinated effort between the Smithsonian Institution and the company, a certain number of protected buildings will be converted for the display of a collection of industrial objects (the Smithsonian houses more than 140 million), thus giving birth to a new national museum of industrial history. The plan offers several advantages: the vast scale of the preserved buildings will make it possible to install very large equipment and machines, and the proximity of Bethlehem to New York and Philadelphia will help make it a tourist destination. Among the attractions will be locomotives and a cannon sixty-five feet long and weighing sixty-five tons, which was part of a Mississippi battleship and has been returned to the site of its manufacture. As the journalist Doug Stewart notes, "tourism has become Pennsylvania's second industry."

This ambitious undertaking does not mean that all the industrial dinosaurs of Bethlehem will escape demolition and the scrap heap. The rescue of Sloss Furnaces in Birmingham represents an exception and not the rule. But that eventuality again raises the question of the irreplaceable nature of the evidence such sites contain, by virtue of their enormous dimensions. That evidence is relevant to understanding an episode that was essential to the history of the country's industrial supremacy, the production of iron and steel. The surviving structures are key physical reminders of the scale of the phenomenon, and, indirectly, its socioeconomic significance. The head of the Department of History and Technology at the National Museum of American History in Washington, D.C., recalls nostalgically: "The steel works were full of fire, heat, and motion." The noise, odors, and heat that are part of that industrial culture have already disappeared. We will undoubtedly have to find the means to replicate, as a demonstration, the manufacturing process, in order to make future generations understand what steel production entailed.

Johnstown's Cambria Iron Company, the pioneering steel-making enterprise of the 1860s, was created under the pressure of demand during the Civil War. It also preserves impressive architectural traces of an activity that ended two decades ago, in particular, an 1864 octagonal brick forge and a machine construction shop dating from 1906. At the time the factories were shut down, the National Park Service was in the process of investing in the creation of Lowell's historic district; it did not dare repeat the operation at the scale of Johnstown's iron and steel industry.

The Monongahela Valley employed eighty thousand steel workers fifty years ago; there were barely four thousand left in 1990. Its historic center is the city of Homestead, which provided steel for the Empire State Building and for the Sears Tower in Chicago. But the Homestead Works closed in the early 1980s, the buildings were scrapped, and the site is no longer notable except as a miserable wasteland. A thirteen-hundred-ton hydraulic press, which forged armor plating for generations of warships, stands in Homestead. The guardians of the memory of a high point in the history of labor (the 1892 Battle of Homestead, during which the workers furiously resisted the assault of strikebreakers) have dismantled a rolling mill and preserved it in detached parts; they hope to reassemble it in a building saved from demolition. For them, and for the survivors of this workforce, saving the memory of "Big Steel" is not only a matter of preserving a technological memory. It is important to remember that people built industry; it did not happen by itself.

Many Americans share an enthusiasm for their local heritage, and they are to be admired for their dedication and tenacity toward preservation issues. That enthusiasm has already advanced the conviction that the industrial heritage is certainly an essential part of American national identity, and this has made it possible to develop a range of solutions for its protection, preservation, and utilization, solutions that offer ideas and models for other industrialized nations wishing to undertake similar projects. It is on the foundation of citizens' initiatives—as well as the efforts of local authorities—that the best chance for government intervention lie. This involvement may be at the federal government level, but more likely it will come from the state level, where the real decision making in matters of historic preservation occurs.

In conclusion, it is useful to summarize the major typological characteristics of these solutions. Many of the "classical" sites illustrating the first phases of American industrialization have been turned into museums, the formulas for which were previously tested in other fields and in other subjects. These museums often take the form of parks, sometimes managed by the state, and sometimes by the federal government through the National Park Service. Their greatest virtues are, in addition to careful restoration, the high quality of information and interpretation that they offer the public, even though these are sometimes marked by a rather insistent pedagogical and/or patriotic concern. Several examples, which are very different in the scope, are: the modest wool-working factory in Watkins Glen, Missouri; the Eleutherian Mills park in Wilmington, Delaware, established by the Hagley Foundations to celebrate the first Du Pont de Nemours plant in the United States; and the creation of the museum and village of Greenfield in Dearborn, Michigan, by Henry Ford I.

Ever since the great wave of deindustrialization and the acceleration of urban changes that swept through the United States in the second half of the twentieth century, the country has become more aware of the irreparable cultural losses it risks incurring and has demonstrated its ability to come up with some innovative solutions to the treatment of large industrial wastelands. However, designated "historic industrial districts" and "industrial heritage corridors" remain, despite the successes, exceptional cases. More effective, no doubt, is adaptive reuse, whose aim is to fully reintegrate the architectural industrial heritage into the urban fabric, while respecting its authenticity. The initiatives that have turned that heritage into commercial shopping centers, hotels, restaurants, and so on generally have demonstrated a great deal of success. A case in point is the only beautiful historic train station preserved in Chicago, Dearborn Station. Other examples involve two of the countless textile factories in the eastern United States: in Bridgeport, Connecticut, one of the cities most damaged by the industrial crisis, an old factory is now a brewery with a courtyard and terraces for its customers; and, in

Baltimore, a hotel chain has taken over a classical spinning mill located near the port. Another formula, with less reliable and less immediate success, consists of offering space for rent or for sale to small or mid-sized businesses.

Most common is the fashion for the conversion of industrial loft buildings into apartments, a use well suited to the size and modularity that were generally characteristic of these structures until the early twentieth century. This solution is so popular that the term *loft* has entered everyday language. These lofts survive today as prestigious buildings for a wealthy clientele, and they can be found at the core of most industrial metropolises in the United States and Europe.

For better or worse, a phase of our material civilization that seems to have passed, after leaving some of the most significant marks on the landscape, is today recognized and respected in the United States. Increasingly, the public is developing an attachment to and fondness toward industrial monuments and landscapes, whose significant contributions are beginning to be better understood and appreciated as the elements of a heritage that has something to offer to the future of our collective history.

Conclusion

In concluding this book, we are left with the impression of incompleteness. This is unavoidable, given that the industrial heritage of the United States, as it has emerged in the last twenty or thirty years of deindustrialization—as industry has been modified and reorganized—is extraordinarily rich, and that the inventory of this heritage remains incomplete, despite the proliferation of research being conducted at the local and regional levels.

That richness is a reflection of the diversity of forms taken by industrialization in the United States during its two major phases, and also of the changes in the human and geographical conditions of industrial expansion in the course of that history. In the northeastern part of the country, the age and relative density of rural settlements, as well as the variety of professional resources in metropolises such as New York and Philadelphia, fostered a certain predominance of small and mid-sized family-type businesses; to the west of the Appalachian Mountains, however, the impact of the industrial explosion after the Civil War, the nature and distribution of raw materials, and the waves of migration favored the development of gigantic capitalistic businesses.

Broad geographical regions have remained relatively unaffected by industrialization, however, especially in the South, where the industrial district of Birmingham, Alabama, an exceptionally powerful center, was hardly representative of the region's economic and social environment. Paradoxically, the unevenness of the industrialization process in different regions suggests a comparison between the United States and Europe, once differences in scale are set aside. That unevenness also applies to the knowledge and preservation of the physical evidence of industrialization prior to the end of World War II. In this case, however, it is considerations of an institutional nature, or the urgency of the situation, or even the dynamics of the various states that account for the differences.

The lesson to be drawn from this modest and overly selective survey is undoubtedly twofold. First, there is a lesson in scholarship: the methods used by the National Park Service in scientifically studying, recording, highlighting, and photographing the material are rigorous and exemplary when compared to those employed on the European continent and in Great Britain. Second, there is a lesson in dedication: segments of American society have proven capable of mobilizing to enact public policies favoring the industrial heritage, and they have found creative solutions of preservation and reuse, applying not only to isolated monuments but to urban planning as a whole. One should seek inspiration from the overview provided in the previous pages and begin to collect data on the most important sites of the industrial heritage throughout the world.

Index

282

284

Bibliography

The photographs that form the framework for this book are taken primarily from the collections of the Historic American Engineering Record (HAER) and, occasionally, from the Historic American Buildings Survey (HABS). As for the rest, they belong to the Hagly Museum and Library; to the American photographers Joseph Elliott, Jet Lowe (who works primarily for the HAER), Sandy Noyes, and Gerald Weinstein; to Albert Kahn Associates (AKA); to the Henry Ford Museum; and to the authors.

The printed sources are composed primarily of: 1) historical studies compiled by American specialists for the HAER's research work and surveys; and 2) the complete collections of the *Journal of the Society for Industrial Archeology* (IA), and of the *Society for Industrial Archeology Newsletter*.

The only current American text in this field is Robert B. Gordon and Patrick M. Malone, *The Texture of Industry: An Archeological View of the Industrialization of North America* (New York and Oxford: Oxford University Press, 1994).

The following were used in preparing this book:

AA. VV. *Industrial Eye.* Photographs by Jet Lowe. Washington, D.C.: Preservation Press, 1986.

———. *Recommendations of the Large Industrial Artifact Advisory Panel, America's Industrial Heritage Project, Pennsylvania.* Denver: Denver Service Center, National Park Service, 1991.

Armstrong, John Borden. *Factory under the Elms: A History of Harrisville, New Hampshire, 1774–1969.* North Andover, Mass.: Museum of American Textile History, 1985.

DeLony, Eric. *Landmark American Bridges.* New York: American Society of Civil Engineers, 1992.

Diamonstein, Barbaralee. *Buildings Reborn: New Uses, Old Places.* Preface by John Brademas. N.p., n.d.

Dilts, James D., and Catharine F. Black, eds. *Baltimore's Cast-Iron Buildings and Architectural Ironwork.* Centreville, Md.: Tidewater, 1991.

Eggert, Gerald, G. *The Iron Industry in Pennsylvania, with a Listing of National, State and Private Sites.* Middletown, Pa.: Pennsylvania Historical Association, 1994.

Ferry, William Hawkins. *The Legacy of Albert Kahn.* Detroit: Wayne State University Press, 1987.

Gayle, Margot. *Cast-Iron Architecture in America: The Significance of James Bogardus.* New York and London: W. W. Norton, 1998.

Gross, Laurence F. *The Course of Industrial Decline: The Boott Cotton Mills of Lowell, Massachusetts, 1835–1955.* Baltimore and London: Johns Hopkins University Press, 1993.

McGaw, Judith A. *Most Wonderful Machine: Mechanization and Social Change in Berkshire Paper Making, 1801–1885.* Princeton: Princeton University Press, 1984.

Marston, Christopher H., ed. *Guidebook to the Pittsburgh Region.* Pittsburgh: Three Rivers Chapter, 1993.

Oliver Evans Chapter of the Society for Industrial Archeology. *Workshop of the World: A Selective Guide to the Industrial Archeology of Philadelphia.* Philadelphia: Oliver Evans, 1990.

Perrin, Noel, and Kenneth Breisch. *Mills and Factories of New England.* With photographs by Serge Hambourg. New York: Harry N. Abrams, Inc., 1988.

Prairie Passage. Photographs by Edward Ranney. Prologue by Tony Hiss. Essays by Emily J. Harris. Epilogue by William Least Heat Moon. Urbana and Chicago: University of Illinois Press, 1998.

Zembala, Dennis M., ed. *Baltimore: Industrial Gateway on the Chesapeake Bay.* Baltimore: Baltimore Museum of Industry, 1995.

Zink, Clifford W., and Dorothy White Hartman. *Spanning the Industrial Age: The John A. Roebling's Sons Company, Trenton, New Jersey, 1848–1974.* Trenton: Trenton Roebling Community Development Corporation, 1992.

Photograph Credits

2: J. Elliott, 1992. 4–5: Hagley Museum & Library. 6–7: J. Elliott, 1993. 8: Jet Lowe for H.A.E.R. 12: Jet Lowe for H.A.E.R., 1984. 15: L. Bergeron, 1998. 17: J. Elliott, 1999. 20: Jack E. Boucher for H.A.E.R., 1974. 22 top: Jack E. Boucher for H.A.E.R., 1973; bottom: David Sharpe for H.A.E.R., 1977. 23: J. Elliott, 1993. 24–25: Jet Lowe for H.A.E.R., 1985. 26–27: Jet Lowe for H.A.E.R., 1978. 28: Jet Lowe for H.A.E.R., 1982. 32 top: L. Bergeron, 1993; bottom: S. Noyes, 1994. 33: L. Bergeron, 1993. 34: L. Bergeron, 1998. 35: L. Bergeron, 1998. 38–39: L. Bergeron, 1996. 40: Jack E. Boucher for H.A.E.R., 1971. 41 bottom left: L. Bergeron, 1997; top and bottom right: Jack E. Boucher for H.A.B.S., 1969. 44: L. Bergeron, 1998. 45 top: Jack E. Boucher for H.A.E.R., 1973; bottom: L. Bergeron. 46–47: H.A.E.R. 47: Jack E. Boucher for H.A.E.R., 1976. 48 top left: Jack E. Boucher for H.A.E.R., 1973; bottom left: H.A.E.R. 48–49: Jack E. Boucher for H.A.E.R., 1976. 50: Randolph Langenbach for H.A.B.S., 1967. 51 top: Jack E. Boucher for H.A.E.R., 1971; bottom: David Sharpe for H.A.E.R., 1977. 53 top: Hagley Museum & Library; bottom: L. Bergeron, 1993. 56: Jet Lowe for H.A.E.R. 61: L. Bergeron, 1998. 62: collection H.A.E.R., from Harpers Weekly, February 26, 1887. 63: Jet Lowe for H.A.E.R., 1978. 64: Jack E. Boucher for H.A.E.R., 1968. 65: Jack E. Boucher for H.A.E.R., 1968. 66 top: Randolph Langenbach for H.A.B.S., 1967; bottom: L. Bergeron, 1997. 67: Hagley Museum & Library. 68 top left: Hagley Museum & Library; top right and bottom: L. Bergeron, 1998. 69: L. Bergeron, 1998. 72 top left and bottom left: L. Bergeron, 1998. 72–73: S. Noyes, 1993. 74: H.A.E.R. 75: L. Bergeron, 1998. 76: Hagley Museum & Library. 77: Hagley Museum & Library. 80: Hagley Museum & Library. 81: Hagley Museum & Library. 82: Hagley Museum & Library. 83: Hagley Museum & Library. 84: Hagley Museum & Library. 85: Hagley Museum & Library. 86–87: J. Elliott, 1990. 88 top: J. Elliott, 1993; bottom: J. Elliott, 1997. 89 top left: J. Elliott, 1993; top right: J. Elliott, 1992; bottom: J. Elliott, 1998. 90: Jack E. Boucher for H.A.E.R., 1977. 91: Jack E. Boucher for H.A.E.R., 1977. 92 left: L. Bergeron, 1997. 92–93: Dennett, Muessig, Ryan & Associates Ltd. for H.A.E.R., 1984. 94: Dennett, Muessig, Ryan & Associates Ltd. for H.A.E.R., 1984. 95: photographer unknown, 1964, collection H.A.E.R. 96: L. Bergeron, 1998. 97: Jet Lowe for H.A.E.R., 1995. 98–99: Albert Kahn Associates. 102 top: H.A.E.R.; bottom: L. Bergeron, 1998. 103 top: L. Bergeron, 1998; bottom: Albert Kahn Associates. 104 left: Forster Studio for Albert Kahn Associates. 104–105: Albert Kahn Associates. 108–109: Jet Lowe for H.A.E.R., 1978. 110: Jet Lowe for H.A.E.R. 114 top: Jean-Claude Robert, 1988; bottom: H.A.E.R. 115 top left: L. Bergeron, 1998; bottom left: L. Bergeron, 1993; right: Jack E. Boucher for H.A.E.R., 1971. 116: Cervin Robinson for H.A.E.R. 117: Cervin Robinson for H.A.B.S. 118 top: William E. Barrett H.A.E.R., 1971; bottom: L. Bergeron, 1998. 119: H.A.B.S. 120: William Edmund Barrett for H.A.E.R. 121: Jack E. Boucher for H.A.E.R. 122: William E. Barrett for H.A.E.R., 1970. 125 top: Jack E. Boucher for H.A.E.R., 1971; bottom: H.A.E.R. 126: Jack E. Boucher for H.A.E.R., 1971. 127 top left and bottom left: L. Bergeron, 1998; right: Jack E. Boucher for H.A.E.R. 128–129: H.A.E.R. 129 right: Jack E. Boucher for H.A.E.R. 130 top: L. Bergeron, 1998; bottom: H.A.E.R. 131: Jet Lowe for H.A.E.R., 1987. 132 top left: L. Bergeron, 1993; bottom left: David Sharpe for H.A.E.R., 1977. 132–133: Jet Lowe for H.A.E.R., 1991. 138: Jet Lowe for H.A.E.R., 1986. 139: Jet Lowe for H.A.E.R., 1986. 140: Jet Lowe for H.A.E.R. 141 top: Jet Lowe for H.A.E.R.; bottom: Jet Lowe for H.A.E.R., 1984. 142 top: L. Bergeron, 1993; bottom: Jet Lowe for H.A.E.R., 1984. 143: Jet Lowe for H.A.E.R., 1983. 144: Jack E. Boucher for H.A.E.R., 1978. 145: Jack E. Boucher for H.A.E.R., 1974. 146 top: Hagley Museum & Library; bottom: Jack E. Boucher for H.A.E.R., 1979. 147 top left: L. Bergeron, 1993; top right: L. Bergeron, 1998; bottom: Jet Lowe for H.A.E.R., 1990. 150: L. Bergeron, 1993. 151 top: Jet Lowe for H.A.E.R., 1985; bottom left and bottom right: Jet Lowe for H.A.E.R., 1990. 152 left: Jet Lowe for H.A.E.R., 1990. 152–153: Jet Lowe for H.A.E.R., 1990. 156 top: collection H.A.E.R., 1975; bottom: L. Bergeron, 1997. 157 top: Jack E. Boucher for H.A.E.R., 1975; bottom: L. Bergeron, 1997. 158: L. Bergeron, 1996. 162: Jet Lowe for H.A.E.R., 1981. 166: collection H.A.E.R., 1978. 167 top: H.A.E.R., 1978; bottom: Jet Lowe for H.A.E.R., 1978. 168 top: Jet Lowe for H.A.E.R., 1978; bottom: H.A.E.R. 169: Jet Lowe for H.A.E.R., 1979. 170 left: Paul Anderson for H.A.E.R., 1987. 170–171: Jet Lowe for H.A.E.R., 1985. 172: Sandy Noyes, 1987. 173: Jet Lowe for H.A.E.R., 1986. 174 top left, top right and center: Jet Lowe for H.A.E.R., 1985; bottom left and bottom right: L. Bergeron, 1998. 175 top: Jet Lowe for H.A.E.R., 1978; bottom: Hagley Museum & Library. 178: Hagley Museum & Library. 179: Jet Lowe for H.A.E.R.,

1981. 180 left: Gerald Weinstein, 1982; top right and bottom right: Gary Samson for H.A.E.R., 1982. 184: Cervin Robinson for H.A.B.S., 1962. 188: Jet Lowe for H.A.E.R., 1990. 189: Jet Lowe for H.A.E.R., 1990. 190: Jet Lowe for H.A.E.R., 1982. 191 top left: Jet Lowe for H.A.E.R., 1979; top right: L. Bergeron, 1991; bottom: H.A.B.S. 192: L. Bergeron, 1993. 193: L. Bergeron, 1993. 194: L. Bergeron, 1993. 195: Gerald Weinstein for H.A.E.R., 1988. 196: L. Bergeron, 1998. 197 top: Joseph Elliott, 1992; bottom: H.A.E.R. 198–199: Hedrich-Blessing for Albert Kahn Associates. 200–201: Hedrich-Blessing for Albert Kahn Associates. 203: William Edmund Barrett for H.A.E.R., 1973. 204 top: L. Bergeron, 1993; bottom left: L. Bergeron, 1998; bottom right: L. Bergeron, 1997. 205: Jack E. Boucher and William E. Barrett for H.A.E.R. 206 left and top right: Piaget-Van Ravensway for H.A.B.S., 1942; bottom right: L. Bergeron, 1990. 207: Piaget-Van Ravensway for H.A.B.S., 1942. 208: L. Bergeron, 1998. 209 top: L. Bergeron, 1998; top left: H.A.E.R.; bottom left and bottom right: L. Bergeron, 1998. 210 top left: L. Bergeron, 1998; bottom left: J. Elliott, 1999. 210–211: Gerald Weinstein. 214–215: Jet Lowe for H.A.E.R., 1978. 216: Jack E. Boucher for H.A.E.R., 1976. 220: Jet Lowe for H.A.E.R., 1988. 221: Jet Lowe for H.A.E.R., 1988.

222: H.A.E.R. 223: H.A.E.R. 224: L. Bergeron, 1998. 225: L. Bergeron, 1998. 228: Hagley Museum & Library. 229 top: Hagley Museum & Library; bottom left and bottom right: L. Bergeron, 1998. 230 left: H.A.E.R. 230–231: H.A.E.R. 232: Gerald Weinstein. 233 top: Jet Lowe for H.A.E.R., 1985; bottom: L. Bergeron, 1998. 234 top: Sandy Noyes, 1993; bottom: L. Bergeron, 1998. 235 top: Sandy Noyes, 1985; bottom left and bottom right: L. Bergeron, 1998. 236 left: Joseph Elliott, 1995. 236–237: Joseph Elliott, 1995. 239 top: L. Bergeron, 1998; bottom: Gerald Weinstein. 240 top: H.A.E.R.; bottom: L. Bergeron, 1998. 244: Jet Lowe for H.A.E.R. 248–249: Jet Lowe for H.A.E.R. 250: L. Bergeron, 1989. 251: L. Bergeron, 1998. 252 top and bottom left: L. Bergeron, 1993; bottom right: L. Bergeron, 1997. 253: L. Bergeron, 1993. 256 top: L. Bergeron, 1997. 257: L. Bergeron, 1997. 258 top left and bottom left: L. Bergeron, 1998. 258–259: Jack E. Boucher for H.A.E.R., 1978. 260: L. Bergeron, 1998. 261: L. Bergeron, 1998. 263: L. Bergeron, 1998. 264: L. Bergeron, 1997. 265: L. Bergeron, 1998. 267: Jack E. Boucher for H.A.E.R., 1974. 268 left: Jet Lowe for H.A.E.R., 1978. 268–269: Jet Lowe for H.A.E.R., 1978. 272: Hagley Museum & Library. 273: Hagley Museum & Library. 274: L. Bergeron, 1998. 275: L. Bergeron, 1998. 276: L. Bergeron, 1998.

Acknowledgments

This book would never have come into being without the collaboration and help of Eric DeLony, director of the Historic American Engineering Record, and of his staff (especially Richard O'Connor and Jet Lowe). The Hagly Museum and Library generously opened its photographic archives, thanks to the interest that Glenn Porter and Roger Horowitz, and the heads of the Pictorial Section, had in our project. Many colleagues provided a direct knowledge of the field, which is irreplaceable for such a study: Robert Billington (for Rhode Island), John Davis, Stephen Victor (for Connecticut), Robert Forster and Edward Papenfuse (for Maryland), Charles K. Hyde, Jean-Claude Robert (for Detroit), and Emory Kemp (for West Virginia and Pennsylvania). The art photographers Joseph Elliott, Sandy Noyes, and Gerald Weinstein have contributed their enormous talent to this book, and we have benefited from their sensitivity to the sites and monuments of American industry that were captured by their lenses, a sensitivity we have come to share.

This project began as an exhibition for the Ecomusée du Creusot-Montceau les Mines, organized by the staff at the Musée de l'Homme et de l'Industrie; it then traveled to Paris, with the patronage and support of Dominique Ferriot, director of the Musée des Arts et Métiers, and of Pierre Aidenbaum, mayor of the Third Arrondissement in Paris.

Dominique Carré, currently the director of Editions du Patrimoine in Paris, was the driving force behind the transformation and expansion of the exhibit into the present book.

Editor, English-language edition: Elisa Urbanelli
Design Coordinator, English-language edition: Tina Thompson

Library of Congress Cataloging-in-Publication Data

Bergeron, Louis, 1929–
    [Patrimoine industriel des Etats-Unis. English]
    Industry, architecture, and engineering : American
ingenuity, 1750–1950 / by Louis Bergeron and Maria Teresa
Maiullari-Pontois ; foreword by Eric DeLony ; translated by
Jane Marie Todd.
      p. cm.
    Includes index.
    1. Industrial engineering—United States. 2. Architecture,
Modern—United States. I. Maiullari-Pontois, Maria Teresa.
II. Title.

NA6402.B4713 2000
609'.73—dc21

00–25279

English translation copyright © 2000 Harry N. Abrams, Inc.
Copyright © 2000 Editions Hoëbeke
Published in 2000 by Harry N. Abrams, Incorporated, New York
All rights reserved. No part of the contents of this book may be
reproduced without the written permission of the publisher.

Printed and bound in Italy

Harry N. Abrams, Inc.
100 Fifth Avenue
New York, N.Y. 10011
www.abramsbooks.com

Riley

St. Louis Community College
at Meramec
Library